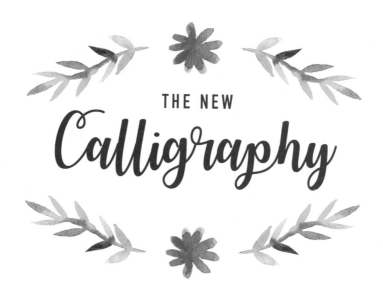

THE NEW

Calligraphy

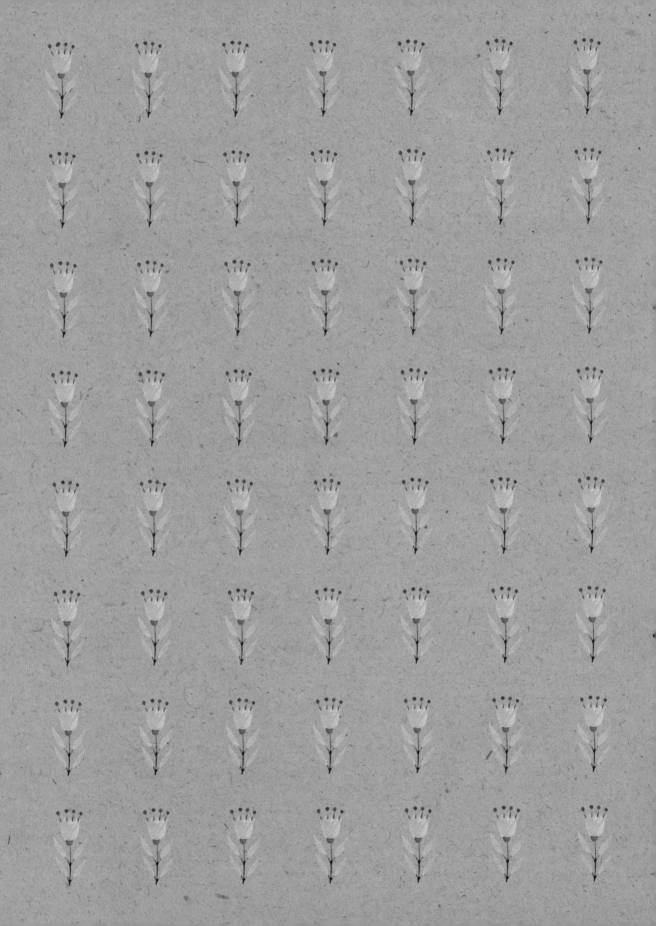

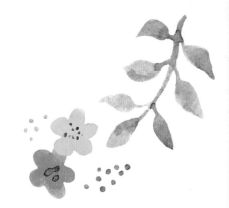

THE NEW
Calligraphy

RUTH BOOTH

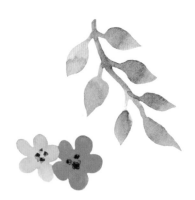

HERBERT PRESS
LONDON · OXFORD · NEW YORK · NEW DELHI · SYDNEY

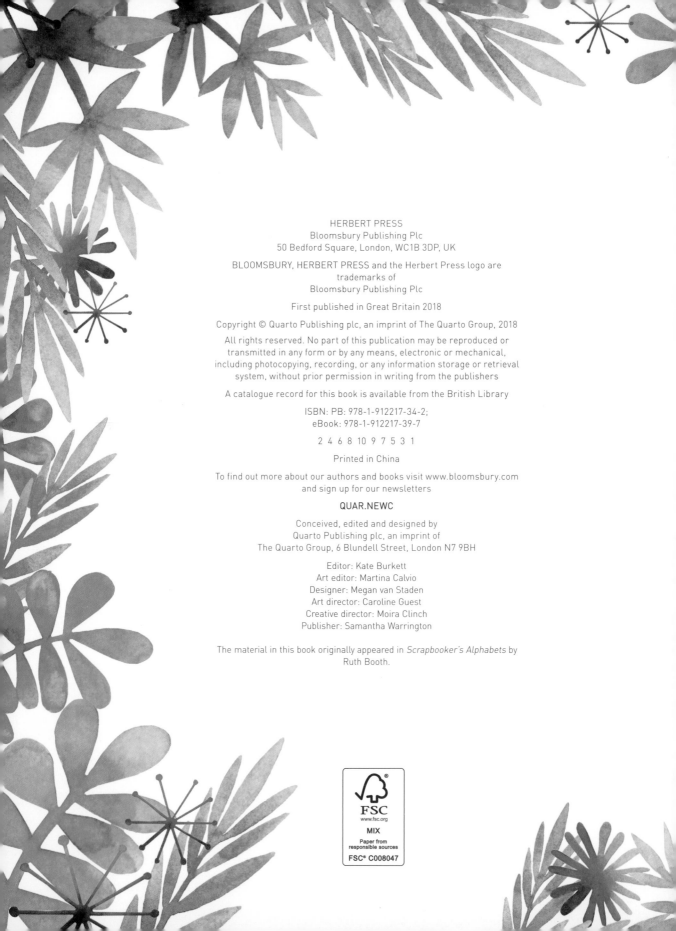

HERBERT PRESS
Bloomsbury Publishing Plc
50 Bedford Square, London, WC1B 3DP, UK

BLOOMSBURY, HERBERT PRESS and the Herbert Press logo are
trademarks of
Bloomsbury Publishing Plc

First published in Great Britain 2018

Copyright © Quarto Publishing plc, an imprint of The Quarto Group, 2018

A catalogue record for this book is available from the British Library

ISBN: PB: 978-1-912217-34-2;
eBook: 978-1-912217-39-7

2 4 6 8 10 9 7 5 3 1

Printed in China

To find out more about our authors and books visit www.bloomsbury.com
and sign up for our newsletters

QUAR.NEWC

Conceived, edited and designed by
Quarto Publishing plc, an imprint of
The Quarto Group, 6 Blundell Street, London N7 9BH

Editor: Kate Burkett
Art editor: Martina Calvio
Designer: Megan van Staden
Art director: Caroline Guest
Creative director: Moira Clinch
Publisher: Samantha Warrington

The material in this book originally appeared in *Scrapbooker's Alphabets* by
Ruth Booth.

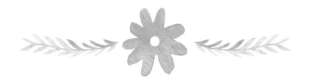

CONTENTS

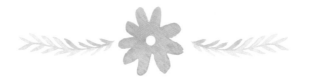

ABOUT THIS BOOK

Each of the 40 alphabets is presented in the same clear
format so that you can easily find the information required
to re-create them.

INTRODUCTION
A brief introduction
to the alphabet,
including ideas
for application.

LETTER HEIGHT
The little black rectangles
shown at the beginning of
some alphabet exemplars
are pen nib widths. These
are used to determine the
height of calligraphic
letters (see pages 8–9).

DOMINANT PEN ANGLE
The dominant pen angle
is the angle at which the
pen is held most of the
time for a calligraphic
alphabet style (see Pen-
angle changes, opposite).

TOOLS
The tools used
to create the
exemplar, plus
alternative
suggestions
(see pages
10–11).

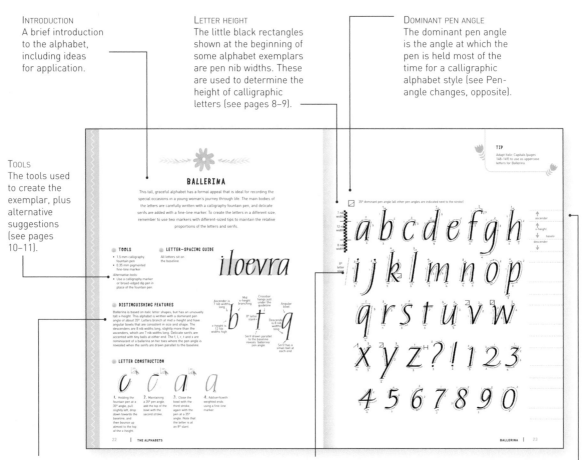

DISTINGUISHING FEATURES
Letter shapes within an
alphabet need to share a
number of characteristics in
order to look like they belong
together. Each alphabet
includes a written description
of its shape, proportions and
characteristics, and is
accompanied by labelled
examples to illustrate
those features.

SLANT LINE
A slant line is shown at the
beginning of an alphabet
exemplar whenever an alphabet
is written at a consistent forward
slant. Slant lines have not been
included for either upright
alphabets or playful styles with
letters that tilt forward and back.

GUIDELINE HELPERS
The fine lines at the right
side of each exemplar are
designed to help you rule
accurate guidelines quickly
and easily in your own
scrapbook. The lines on
the subsequent pages of
each alphabet act as a
place for you to practise
your hand lettering.

PEN-ANGLE CHANGES

Pen angles are relevant only to alphabets made with a calligraphic tool. They refer to the angle of the broad edge of the pen tip relative to the baseline or writing line. The dominant angle at which the pen is held for a particular calligraphic alphabet style may need to be changed for certain letter strokes. This is indicated by a small box showing a different pen angle beside the relevant stroke. For instance, a slightly steeper pen angle is usually used to make the first and third diagonal in w so that the weight of those strokes is consistent with the weight of the downstroke in other letters. A very flat pen angle is used for the mid-stroke of the z so that it also has a weight similar to the downstroke of other letters in the alphabet family. Rotate the nib clockwise for steeper pen angles (45–60º) and slightly anticlockwise for flatter pen angles (20–0º).

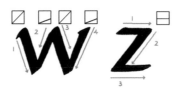

DUCTUS

Grey arrows and numbers are shown beside each stroke of the letters on most alphabet exemplars. This is the ductus. Ductus lines are included whenever the direction and order of the strokes affects the construction of the letters. A certain stroke direction may be recommended because of the nature of the tool being used or because it makes it easier for writers to see what they are doing. Where there are ductus lines without numbers, the direction of the stroke is still important, but the letter is made with one continuous stroke. When drawing letter forms that have no ductus, you may find it helpful to rotate your writing page.

DECORATIVE BORDERS

Each alphabet comes with a decorative border, which allows the calligrapher to add a personal touch to everything, from invitations to scrapbooks, doodles to wedding stationery, journals to posters.

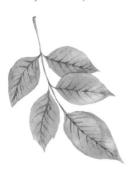

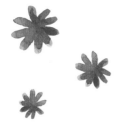

LETTER CONSTRUCTION

Construction instructions for one or two letters are included with each alphabet. Step-by-step drawings are accompanied by written instructions to demonstrate how letter strokes fit together. Each step is shown in black, with any previous strokes shown in grey. Ductus arrows are included to show the direction of the strokes where appropriate. A small image of the tool tip is also included when the position of a calligraphy pen or brush is important. It may be helpful to look at the construction instructions shown for other alphabets made with the same writing tool; just be sure to follow the ductus and pen-angle instructions for the letter style you are doing.

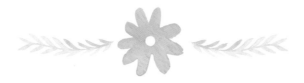

ADJUSTING THE LETTER HEIGHT

The relationship between the pen nib width and the letter height has a significant impact on the appearance of a calligraphic letter style, while monoline and drawn alphabets can be adapted to different sizes fairly easily, often with the same tool.

When lettering a calligraphic alphabet at a different size, you must use a different-sized broad-edged marker or pen nib. The x-height, descenders and ascenders are measured in nib widths. An alphabet with an x-height of 4 nib widths will be smaller when written with a narrower nib and larger when written with a wider nib, but the alphabet's proportions will remain the same.

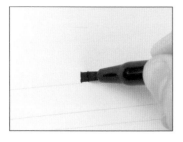
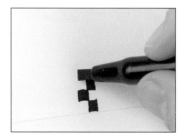
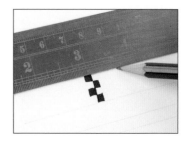

I. Refer to the alphabet exemplar to see how many nib widths the x-height, ascenders and descenders should be. On a piece of scrap paper, draw a baseline. Position your pen or marker so that the width of the nib is at 90º to the baseline. Pull a short horizontal line along the baseline; it will look like a small box. In order to achieve accurate results, it is very important to position the pen nib accurately and pull short straight boxes at 90º to the baseline.

2. Maintain the 90º pen angle and make another little box, making sure that the bottom edge of this box aligns with the top edge of the previous box. Repeat this process until you have the correct number of nib widths, staggering the boxes so that you can identify how many there are.

3. Once the ink is dry, rule a parallel guideline at the top of the staggered stack of nib widths. The distance between these two lines is your new x-height. Determine the ascender and descender heights using the same method.

● MONOLINE AND DRAWN ALPHABETS

When adapting monoline and drawn alphabets to different sizes using the same tool, just be sure to maintain the same letter proportions. If the alphabet has ascenders and descenders that are the same length as its x-height, they should remain the same as the x-height when the lettering is done at a different size. A significant change in alphabet size may require a finer or thicker writing tool.

LETTER SPACING

Letter spacing creates texture on the page. Your lettering will be more pleasing, easier to read and create a more attractive texture if it is spaced appropriately.

LETTER-SPACING GUIDE

The letter-spacing guide has been designed to help you see the appropriate spaces between the letters more easily, while giving you a visual impression of a word written in each alphabet style.

Alphabets with letters of consistent proportion and shape, such as Roman Majuscules (pages 162–165), need to be spaced evenly so that distracting dark areas or white holes are not created within the texture of the lettering.

Uneven spacing is more appropriate for alphabets with inconsistent letter shapes and sizes.

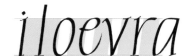

Roman Majuscules
Alphabets with consistent proportions and shapes require even spacing. The blue spacer equals the most difficult letter-spacing combination.

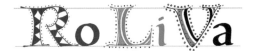

BLUE SPACERS

Alphabets that are more pleasing with consistent spacing have been assigned a standard-sized blue spacer. Lowercase alphabets, such as Ballerina (pages 22–24), have a spacer that is about the same size as the counter space in the n. Uppercase alphabets with letters of classic proportions are given a spacer about equal to the most difficult letter-spacing combination.

For instance, in Roman Majuscules, the LA combination presents a challenge because even when those two letters are tucked closely together, there is still a significant space. The standard spacer varies from one alphabet to another because letter shapes and weights vary. Block letters – an alphabet with letters that are all about the same width, such as Art Deco Capitals (pages 76–79) – are simply placed side by side.

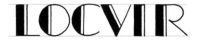

Ballerina
Consistent lowercase alphabets have a spacer equal to the counter space in the n.

LETTER TYPES

The letters featured in the letter-spacing guide have been chosen to demonstrate the relationships between a variety of letter types: straight-sided letters (il), straight and round (lo), round and round (oe), open and diagonal (ev), diagonal and straight (vr), open and round or open (ra). In order to achieve letter spacing that looks reasonably consistent, we need to determine visually where the letter ends and the space between the letters begins. Our eye tends to borrow a portion of the area around and within some letters and add it to the space between the letters. That is why the blue spacer boxes sometimes overlap a portion of the letters.

Art Deco Capitals
Block letters should simply be placed side by side.

WRITING TOOLS

The writing tools used to create the alphabet exemplars in this book are commonly found in most art and craft shops.

1. DOUBLE-ENDED PERMANENT MARKER

Two monoline tools in one: a fine tip at one end and a broad tip at the other. Several brands have pigmented ink and are archival.

2. POINTED BRUSH PEN

This is a pen because it has its own ink cartridge; it is also a brush because it has a real pointed brush tip. It comes in a variety of colours, but it is not permanent or lightfast.

3. INK

Use carbon-based or pigmented ink. Avoid Indian ink and inks that have shellac in them because they may remain sticky.

4. MODIFIED LOLLY STICK

A flat wooden stick about 10 mm (⅜ inch) wide, with one end cut off and sanded smooth. It is used with an ink pad to stamp Stick Letters (pages 104–109).

5. INK PAD

Available in a wide range of colours for rubber stamping. Many are pigmented and archival.

6. CALLIGRAPHY FOUNTAIN PEN

A tool with interchangeable broad-edged tips of different sizes and its own reservoir of ink. The ink in these pens is not lightfast or waterproof.

7. PIGMENTED CALLIGRAPHY MARKER

A marker with a broad-edged tip. There are several archival brands that come in a range of tip widths labelled in millimetres.

8. MEDIUM-POINT PERMANENT MARKER

A monoline tool with a slightly larger tip than the fine-line markers. These are waterproof and lightfast, but may not be acid-free. Note that these markers also come in a variety of colours, but that not all colours are permanent.

9. GEL PEN

A monoline tool that comes in a wide variety of colours and qualities. Some are permanent and acid-free.

10. METALLIC PEN

Metallic inks contain small, finely ground particles, which yield a smooth, even sheen. The 1.0 mm tip is broad enough to glide effortlessly across the page. Still, it lays down fine lines suitable for small letters and details.

11. SOFT WHITE ERASER

Soft, so that it will not damage the paper; white, so that it will not leave a coloured residue.

12. GRAPHITE PENCIL

A common monoline tool with a graphite writing tip that can be sharpened to a point or used dull and rounded. Pencils are graded on a scale from H (hardness) to B (blackness).

Very hard pencils (9H) lay down little graphite and are therefore lighter on the page, but may score the paper. Very soft pencils (9B) lay down more graphite and are therefore darker on the page, but smudge easily. HB indicates the middle of the range.

13. BALLPOINT PEN

Common monoline writing tool with its own ink cartridge. The ink in these pens is not lightfast unless indicated on the label.

14. BROAD-EDGED DIP PEN

Metal broad-edged nibs that fit into a handle. These come in a range of sizes and require a separate ink source.

15. PIGMENTED FINE-LINE MARKER

Monoline tool that comes in a range of fine tips. The rendered line width is shown in millimetres on the label. Most brands are permanent and archival.

16. COLOURED FINE-LINE MARKER

A fine-tipped monoline tool that comes in a wide range of colours. These markers are not permanent or archival unless indicated on the label.

17. COLOURED PENCIL

A monoline tool that can be sharpened to a point or used rounded and dull; available in a range of qualities. Artist-quality offers the richest, most permanent and lightfast colour.

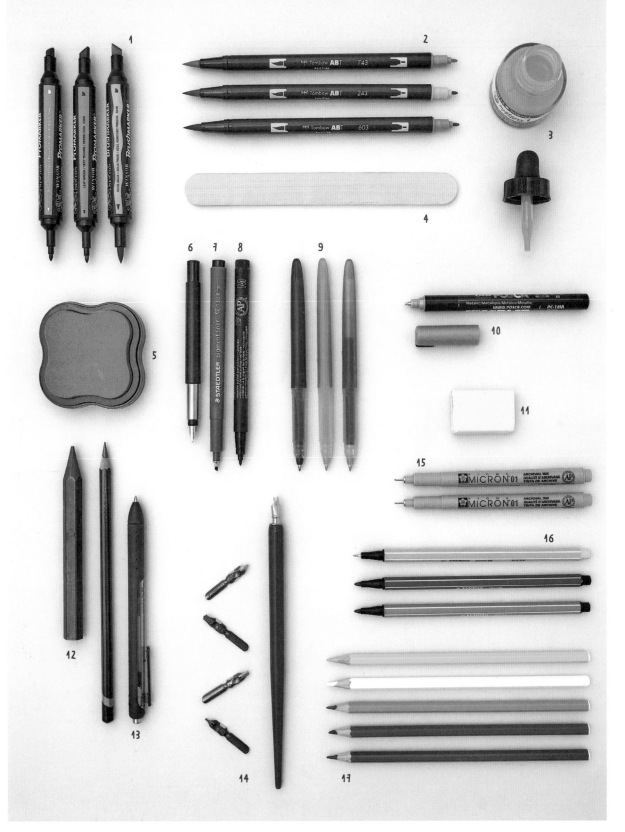

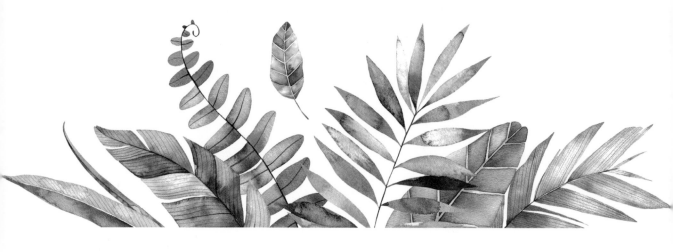

CHAPTER ONE:
THE ALPHABETS

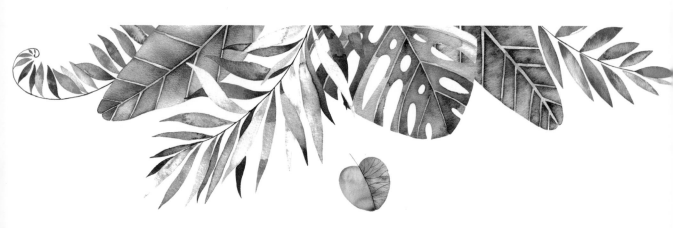

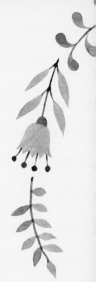

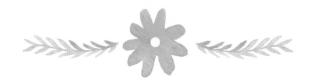

GRANDMA'S HANDWRITING

Nothing looks more sincere than a handwritten note. This alphabet reminds us of a time when personal handwriting was the only way to send a love letter or thank-you note. Follow the exemplar shown opposite and on pages 18–19. Use Grandma's Handwriting for labels or longer heartfelt expressions of love and admiration for those you cherish.

TOOLS

- 0.50 mm pigmented fine-line marker

Alternative tools:
- Pencil, ballpoint pen, coloured pencil or coloured marker

LETTER-SPACING GUIDE

Some letters are not joined.

DISTINGUISHING FEATURES

The letter shapes are generally oval, and although it is a running hand, some letters are not joined. A number of letters include a small curl, and most of the ascenders and descenders are looped. Fairly consistent letter slant and repeated letter shapes make the writing more attractive. There are a number of inconsistencies within this alphabet – a testimony to the unique nature of each person's own handwriting.

Open oval bowl

Inconsistent letter shapes

Descender equals the x-height

Most ascenders and descenders are looped

Left-motion descenders end with a small hook

Some ascenders and descenders have no loop

Most ascenders equal the x-height

30° letter slant

LETTER CONSTRUCTION

1. Begin with a slanted upward stroke, making it slightly curved.

2. Continue around to create a fairly significant top loop.

3. Continue the stroke, making a shoulder and then dropping down towards the baseline on a 30° slant.

4. Exit by pulling right, keeping almost parallel to the baseline.

TIP

Use Grandma's Handwriting Capitals (pages 16–17) as the uppercase letters for this alphabet.

30° letter
slant

/ a b c d e f

ascender
x-height
baseline
descender

g h i j k l

m n o p q r

s t u v w x

y z ! ? / 2 3

4 5 6 7 8 9 0

GRANDMA'S HANDWRITING CAPITALS

These letters should only be used as capital letters with the lowercase Grandma's Handwriting. Large uppercase letters make handwriting more legible and provide welcome resting places in a long body of text. This alphabet features some traditional letter forms, but you can substitute your own if you wish; try to be consistent within a single project. You can use the same tool to write this alphabet in different sizes.

TOOLS

- 0.50 mm pigmented fine-line marker

Alternative tools:

- Pencil, ballpoint pen, coloured pencil or coloured marker

LETTER-SPACING GUIDE

This uppercase alphabet was designed for use only with the lowercase letters, not to be used alone. These three spacing examples demonstrate some upper- and lowercase letters together.

DISTINGUISHING FEATURES

This alphabet is written at a letter slant of approximately 30º. You may be more comfortable with a different slant; what is important is to be fairly consistent. These traditional letters have large oval flourishes, and some have the same small curl at the base of the vertical that is found on the accompanying lowercase alphabet. A number of these letters graduate down towards the right, emphasizing the letter slant.

Familiar old-fashioned letter shapes

Large oval flourish

Some letters graduate downward

30º letter slant

Most letters are drawn without lifting the pen

Inconsistent letter shapes

Some letters have descenders

LETTER CONSTRUCTION

1. Begin by drawing a large oval curl and then a diagonal line at about 30º, extending down to the baseline.

2. Continue with an upward diagonal that ends at about three-quarters of the letter height.

3. Draw another diagonal parallel to the first one.

4. Complete the letter with a curved diagonal extending up to about half the letter height.

TIP

Use Grandma's Handwriting (pages 14–15) as the lowercase letters and numbers for this alphabet.

30° letter slant

Capital height

baseline

A B C D E

F G H I J K

L M N O P

Q R S T U

V W X Y & Z

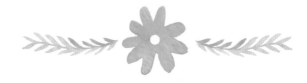

A B C D E F G H I J K L M N

Capital
height

baseline

A A B C D E F G

H I J K L M N

a b c d e f g h i j k l m

ascender

x-height
baseline

descender

a b c d e f g h i j k l m

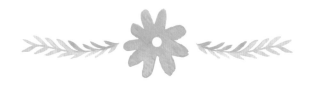

O P 2 R S T U V W X Y & Z

O P 2 R S T U V

W X Y & Z

n o p q r s t u v w x y z

n o p q r s t u v w x y z

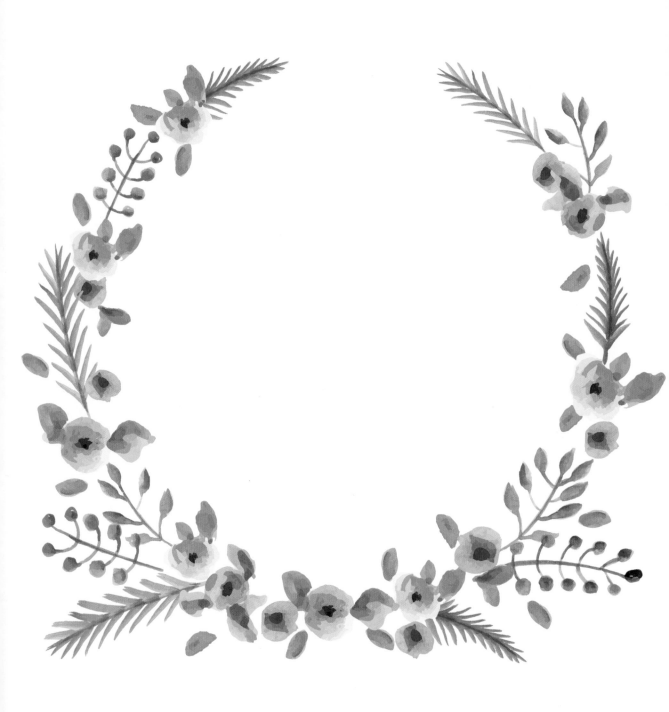

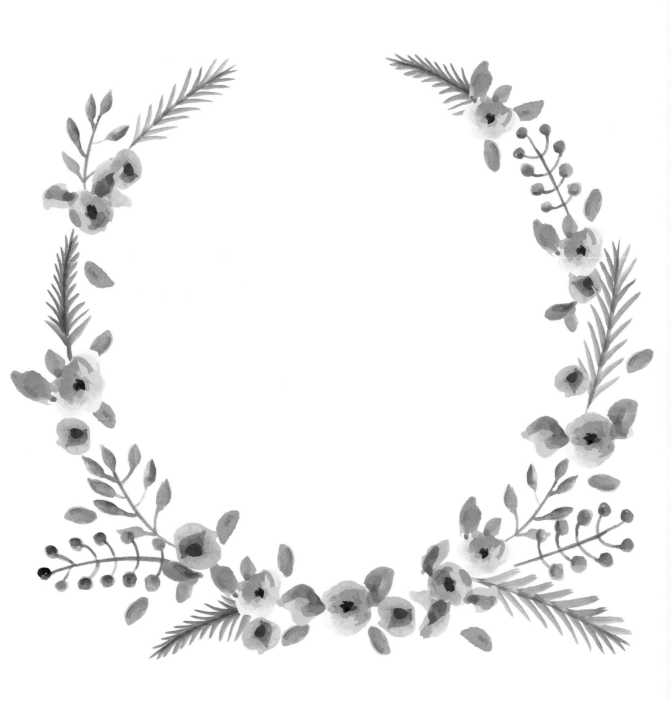

BALLERINA

This tall, graceful alphabet has a formal appeal that is ideal for recording the special occasions in a young woman's journey through life. The main bodies of the letters are carefully written with a calligraphy fountain pen, and delicate serifs are added with a fine-line marker. To create the letters in a different size, remember to use two markers with different-sized tips to maintain the relative proportions of the letters and serifs.

TOOLS

- 1.5 mm calligraphy fountain pen
- 0.35 mm pigmented fine-line marker

Alternative tools:
- Use a calligraphy marker or broad-edged dip pen in place of the fountain pen.

LETTER-SPACING GUIDE

All letters sit on the baseline.

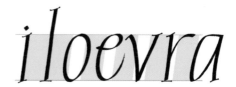

DISTINGUISHING FEATURES

Ballerina is based on italic letter shapes, but has an unusually tall x-height. This alphabet is written with a dominant pen angle of about 35°. Letters branch at mid x-height and have angular bowls that are consistent in size and shape. The descenders are 8 nib widths long, slightly more than the ascenders, which are 7 nib widths long. Delicate serifs are accented with tiny balls at either end. The f, l, r, t and x are reminiscent of a ballerina on her toes where the pen angle is revealed when the serifs are drawn parallel to the baseline.

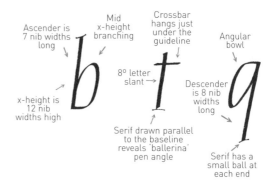

LETTER CONSTRUCTION

1. Holding the fountain pen at a 35° angle, pull slightly left, drop down towards the baseline, and then bounce up almost to the top of the x-height.

2. Maintaining a 35° pen angle, add the top of the bowl with the second stroke.

3. Close the bowl with the third stroke, again with the pen at a 35° angle. Note that the letter is at an 8° slant.

4. Add serifs with weighted ends using a fine-line marker.

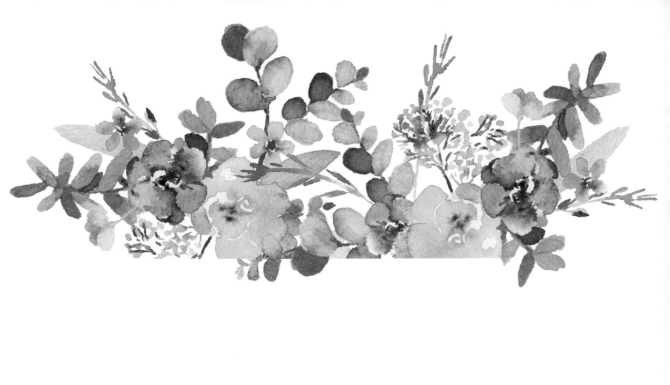

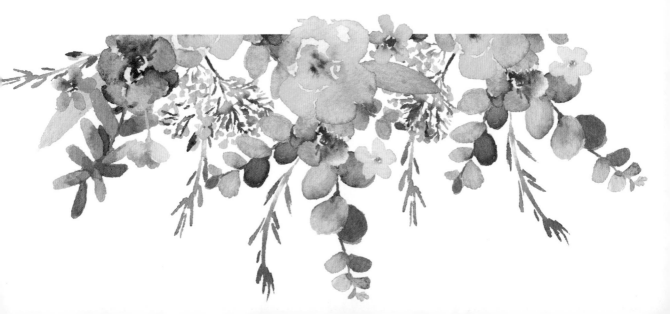

ISABELLA

Inspired by a traditional handwritten script, this alphabet has elegant proportions and a gentle rhythm that make it ideal for greetings cards, picture labels and captions about afternoon tea parties, romantic weekends or church gatherings. Long bodies of text will need a lot of space due to the very long ascenders and descenders. A variety of letter sizes can be achieved using the same writing tool.

⬤ TOOLS

- 0.35 mm pigmented fine-line marker

Alternative tools:
- Pencil, coloured pencil or coloured fine-line marker

⬤ LETTER–SPACING GUIDE

All letters sit on the baseline.

iloevra

⬤ DISTINGUISHING FEATURES

This letter style is written at an extreme slant of 38°. Subtle shading is added to the r, the shortened descender of the p and the elongated t. This provides contrast and helps relate the lowercase letters to the elaborately shaded capitals. Additional interest is created by the unusual crossbar that hovers above the t. These letters are written rhythmically as a continuous script, with looped ascenders and descenders that are almost three times the length of the x-height and consistently shaped oval bowls.

Short x-height ↓

p

Extended exit stroke ↑

Half-length shaded descender

Lead-in stroke | Oval bowl

g

Looped descender is almost three times as long as the x-height

38° letter slant

T

Half-height shaded ascender topped with a separate curved crossbar

⬤ LETTER CONSTRUCTION

r   *d*   *d*   *d*

1. Begin with the lead-in portion of the letter. Note that the letter is on a 38° slant.

2. Continue by drawing the bowl.

3. Retrace halfway up. Continue up the ascender and outline the shaded top. Retrace and extend the ascender down to the baseline. End with the exit stroke.

4. Fill in the shaded top of the ascender.

TIP

Use Isabella Capitals (pages 30–31) as the uppercase letters for this alphabet.

38° letter slant

ascender
x-height · baseline
descender

a b c d e f

g h i j k l

m n o p q r s

T u v w x y z

0 1 2 3 4 5 6 7 8 9 ! ?

ISABELLA CAPITALS

These elaborate letters were inspired by an alphabet traditionally written with a flexible-pointed dip pen. Shading is outlined and filled in where the penman would have added pressure to the pen nib to widen the stroke. Due to its extensive flourishing, only use these capital letters with the lowercase Isabella alphabet rather than alone. This alphabet can easily be adapted to larger lettering without changing the writing tool.

⬤ TOOLS

- 0.35 mm pigmented fine-line marker

Alternative tools:
- Pencil, coloured pencil or coloured fine-line marker

⬤ LETTER-SPACING GUIDE

This uppercase alphabet was designed for use only with the lowercase letters, not to be used alone. These three spacing examples demonstrate some upper- and lowercase letters together.

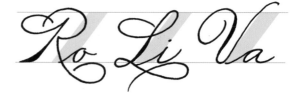

⬤ DISTINGUISHING FEATURES

These large capitals have consistently shaped oval bowls that are echoed by elaborate oval flourishes. Carefully drawn shading accents each of these extravagant letters. All of the letters are drawn fluidly with a long, continuous motion and at an extreme slant of 38°. The exit strokes need to be adjusted to accommodate the lowercase letters that follow them. Practice is needed to draw these capitals consistently.

Upper bowl is larger than lower bowl ↘

Large oval flourishes

38° letter slant

Curves sometimes break through guidelines

Shaded foot

Shading on the curve

Oval counter space

⬤ LETTER CONSTRUCTION

1. Begin the flourish below the top guideline, then complete the first stroke by outlining a small area for shading.

2. Begin the second stroke in the centre of the flourish.

3. Add a small crossbar.

4. Carefully fill in the shaded foot.

TIP

Use Isabella (pages 28–29) as the lowercase letters and numbers for this alphabet.

38° letter slant

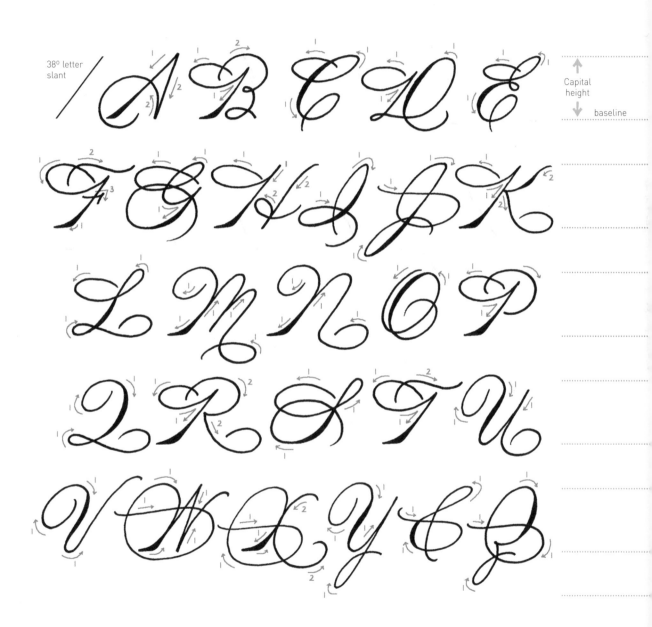

Capital height

baseline

A B C D E F G H I J K L M N

Capital height
↓ baseline

A B C D E F

G H I J K L M N

a b c d e f g h i j k l m

ascender
x-height
baseline
descender

a b c d e f g h

i j k l m

O P Q R S T U V W X Y Z

O P Q R S T U

V W X Y Z

n o p q r s t u v w x y z

n o p q r s t u v w

x y z

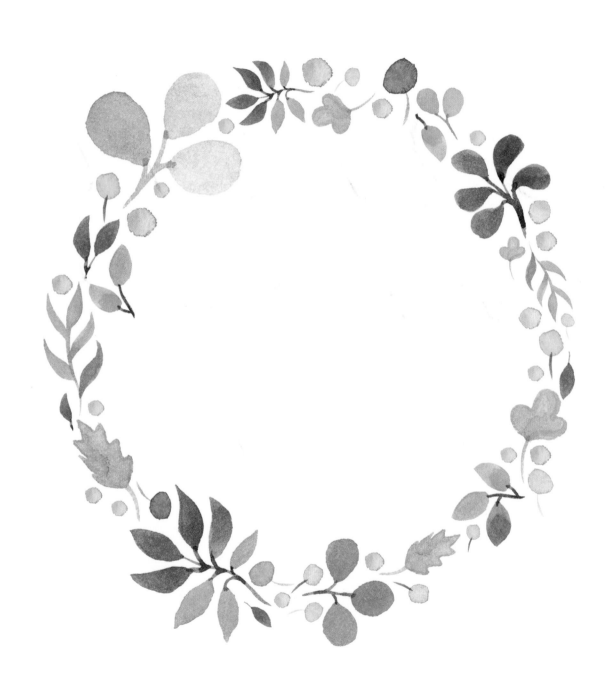

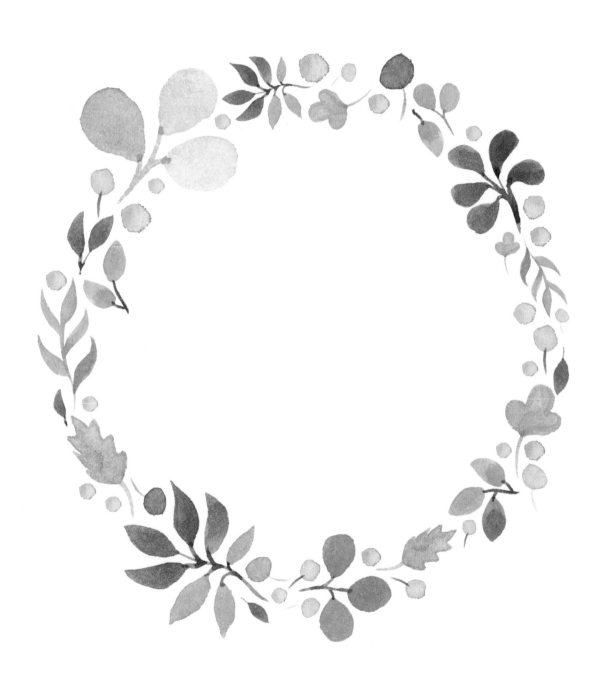

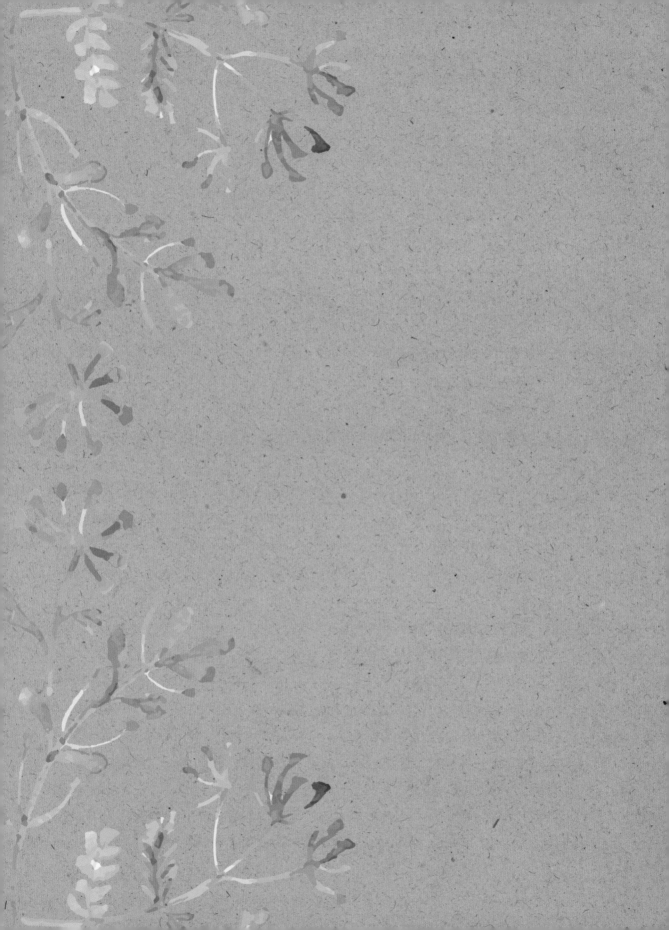

ROMEO

Majestic letter proportions made with a humble writing tool give this alphabet a gentle but honourable appearance. These letters need to be drawn slowly and carefully. Romeo is a fitting alphabet for love poems or captions about your loved one. It is an alphabet you can linger over once those dreams have come true. Use the same tool to draw the letters in a range of sizes.

● TOOLS

- 6B pencil

Alternative tools:
- Coloured pencils

● LETTER-SPACING GUIDE

All letters sit on the baseline.

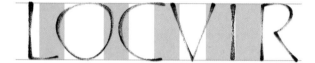

● DISTINGUISHING FEATURES

Each stroke is carefully built up by retracing it several times. Use a pressure–release–pressure technique to create strokes with thinner, lighter midsections. This alphabet has classic proportions and includes signature O and M shapes. Pencil gives the letters a lovely soft texture. The graphite is likely to smudge, so you may want to create this effect purposely using a finger or stub of paper.

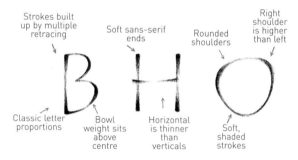

Strokes built up by multiple retracing

Soft sans-serif ends

Rounded shoulders

Right shoulder is higher than left

Classic letter proportions

Bowl weight sits above centre

Horizontal is thinner than verticals

Soft, shaded strokes

● LETTER CONSTRUCTION

I. Using a dull 6B pencil, draw the first stroke so that it leans slightly forward, adding pressure at the start and end, and releasing pressure in the middle.

2. Begin the second stroke with pressure, release, then add pressure as you approach the curve. Release on the way back up. The curve is off-centre and does not meet the baseline.

3. Begin the third stroke with pressure, release, then add pressure again towards the bottom. Note that this stroke leans slightly backward.

4. Retrace the letter using pressure–release–pressure strokes until the letter is as substantial as you want it to be.

TIP

Romeo does not require a coordinating lowercase alphabet.

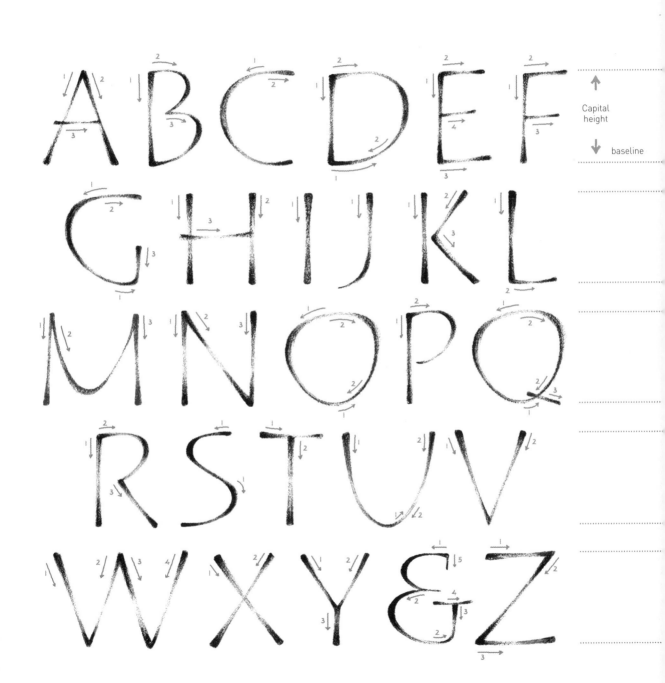

Capital height

baseline

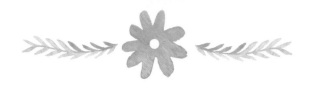

ABCDEFGHIJKLMN

↑
Capital
height

↓ baseline

OPQRSTUVWXY&Z

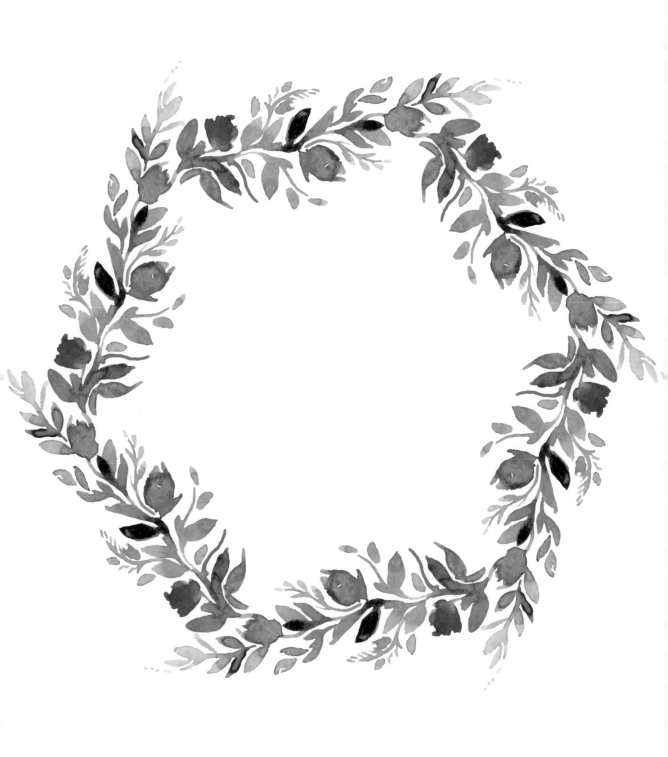

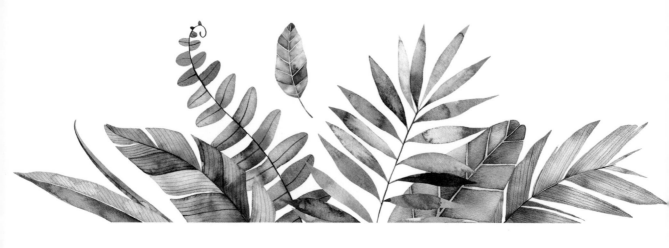

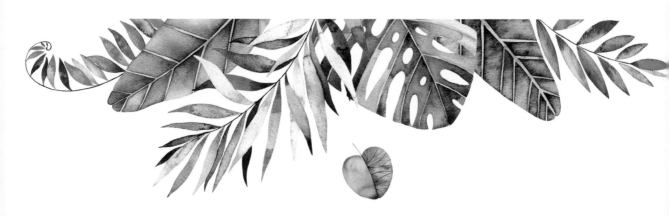

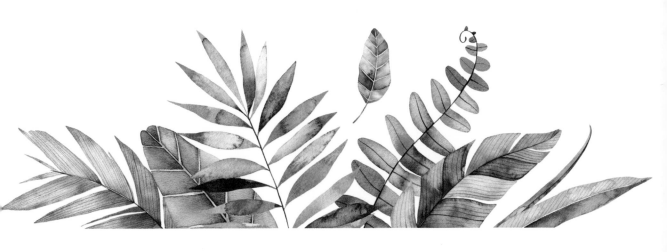

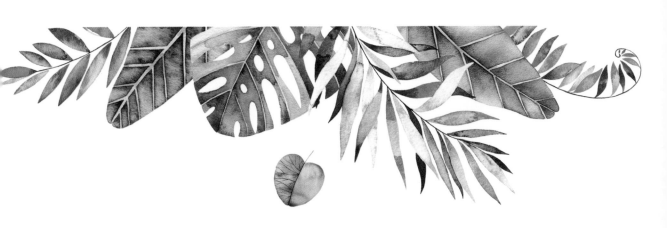

ART NOUVEAU

These slightly unusual, Art Nouveau-inspired letter forms incorporate small oval curls to produce a simple, sweet little alphabet that is easy to use. It is suitable for titles and text about childhood romances or lovable but quirky old friends, or for humorous captions to accompany photos of children dressed up in Grandma's bonnet and high heels. This alphabet can be written at a range of x-heights using the same monoline tool.

TOOLS

- 0.50 mm pigmented fine-line marker

Alternative tools:
- Any monoline writing tool

LETTER-SPACING GUIDE

All letters sit on the baseline.

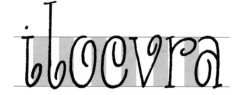

DISTINGUISHING FEATURES

These vertical, high-branching letters have short serifs and oval bowls. The signature feature of the alphabet is the oval curls, which are also found in the accompanying uppercase alphabet. Each letter includes an oval curl, either within the body or as a foot. Take special note of the angle of the oval-curl feet. The body of these letters sits comfortably under the high waist of the uppercase letters, and the ascenders and descenders are slightly shorter than the x-height.

Ascender is slightly shorter than x-height

High branching

Oval-curl foot

Letters are vertical

Oval bowl

Descender is slightly shorter than x-height

Short serif

Oval curl within body of letter

Right side extended slightly to accommodate curl

LETTER CONSTRUCTION

1. Beginning at the top, draw a vertical stroke.

2. Start the second stroke about mid x-height within the first stroke, tracing the first stroke briefly before branching out.

3. Begin the third stroke so that it overlaps the second, making the counter space as wide as the first one at the top, then narrowing it towards the bottom to make room for the curled foot.

4. Add a short serif to the top and bottom of the first stroke.

TIP

Use Art Nouveau Capitals (pages 48–49) as the uppercase letters for this alphabet.

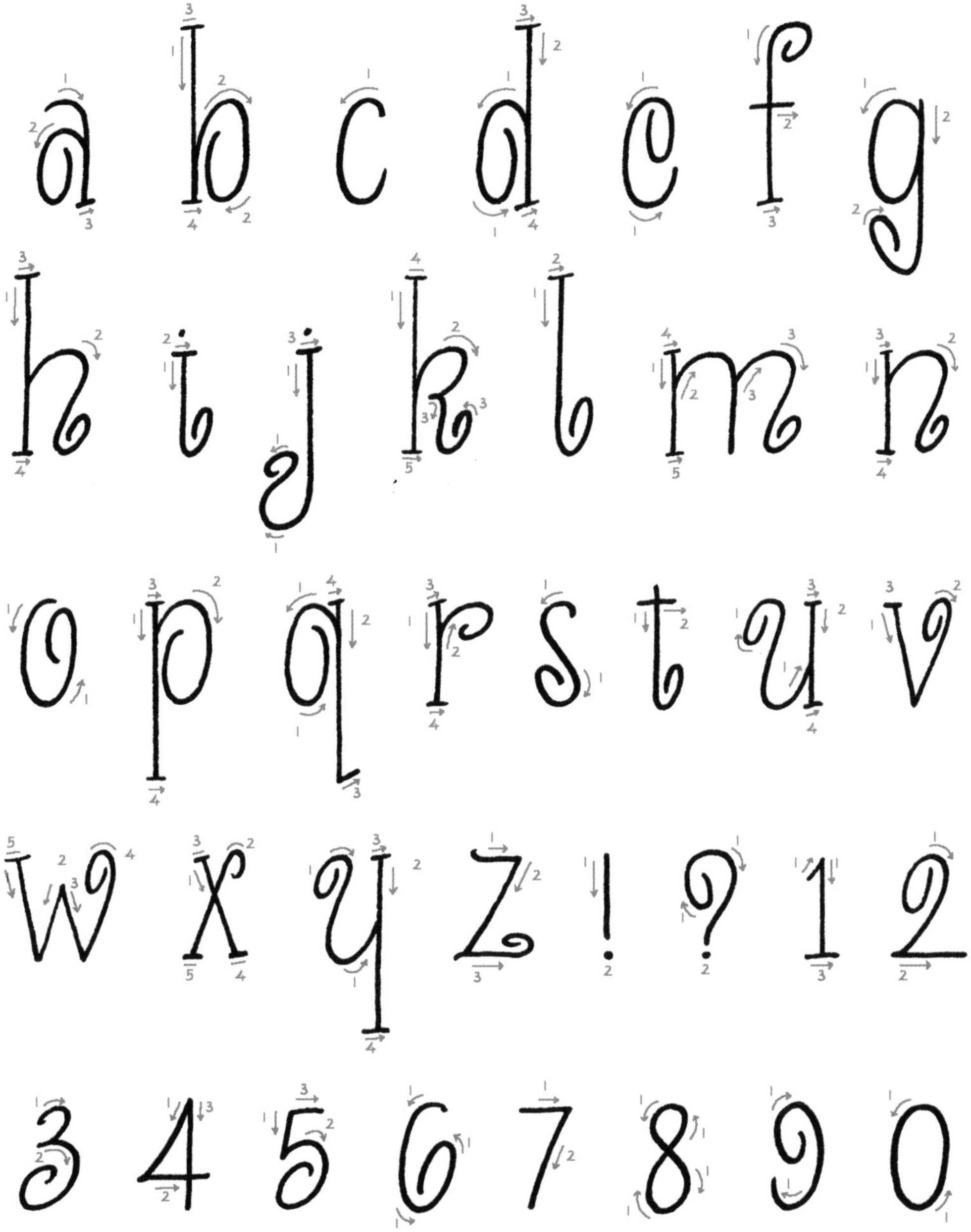

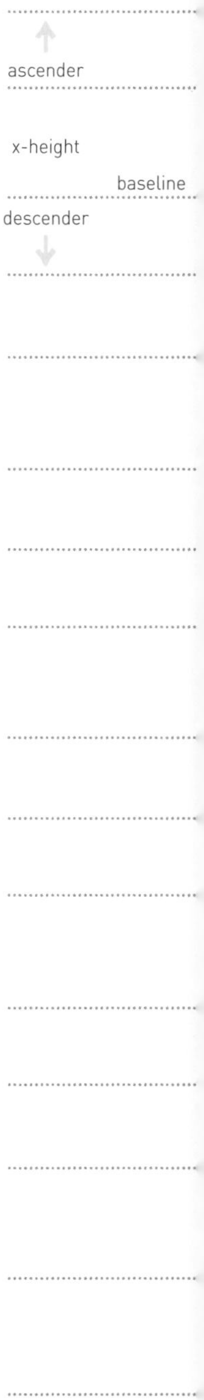

a b c d e f g

ascender

x-height

baseline

descender

h i j k l m n

o p q r s t u v

w x y z ! ? 1 2

3 4 5 6 7 8 9 0

ART NOUVEAU CAPITALS

Inspired by chic Art Nouveau styling, this alphabet has a few eccentric but endearing twists. The letters can be used alone for titles or captions, or with lowercase Art Nouveau for longer bodies of text. The tall, elegant letters have just the right humorous touch for writing romantic comedy stories. The same tools can be used to draw the letters slightly taller; for shorter letters, use a narrower calligraphy marker.

TOOLS

- 0.50 mm pigmented fine-line marker
- 200 pigmented calligraphy marker

LETTER-SPACING GUIDE

All letters sit on the baseline.

DISTINGUISHING FEATURES

These letters are vertical, fairly narrow and consistent in height. They are high waisted and slightly wider at the top than the bottom, with oval-shaped curls of various sizes incorporated into each letter. There is a signature oval-curl foot, reminiscent of old-fashioned iron patio furniture, on the A, K, M and R, and large oval curls within many of the other letter forms. Those oval curls are echoed by the curled serifs that adorn the double-stroked verticals.

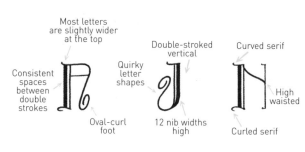

Most letters are slightly wider at the top

Consistent spaces between double strokes

Oval-curl foot

Quirky letter shapes

Double-stroked vertical

12 nib widths high

Curved serif

High waisted

Curled serif

LETTER CONSTRUCTION

I. Beginning at the top, draw a vertical stroke using a fine-line marker.

2. Use a calligraphy marker at a 0° angle to add a parallel stroke. Curve and taper to the left about three-quarters of the way down.

3. Using the fine-line marker, draw an oval curl. End the stroke so that it overlaps the end of the previous stroke.

4. Use the fine-line marker to add a serif.

TIP

Use Art Nouveau (pages 46–47) as the lowercase letters and numbers for this alphabet.

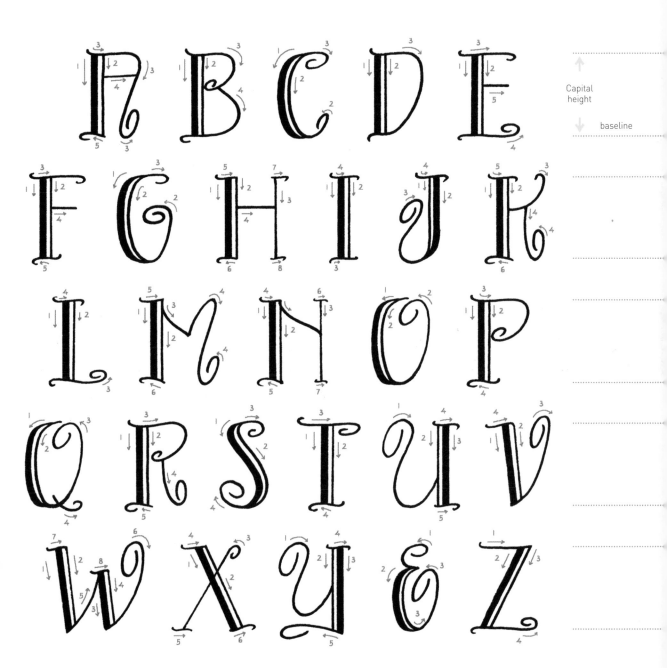

Capital height

baseline

A B C D E F G H I J K L M N

Capital
height

baseline

a b c d e f g h i j k l m

ascender

x-height

baseline

descender

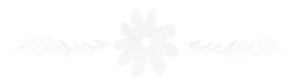

O P Q R S T U V W X Y Z

n o p q r s t u v w x y z

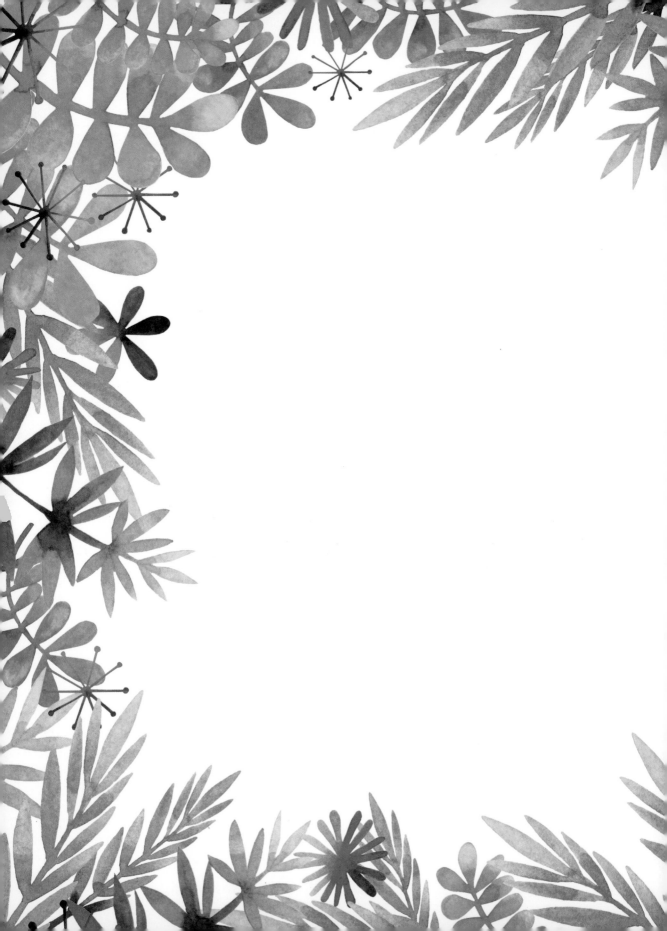

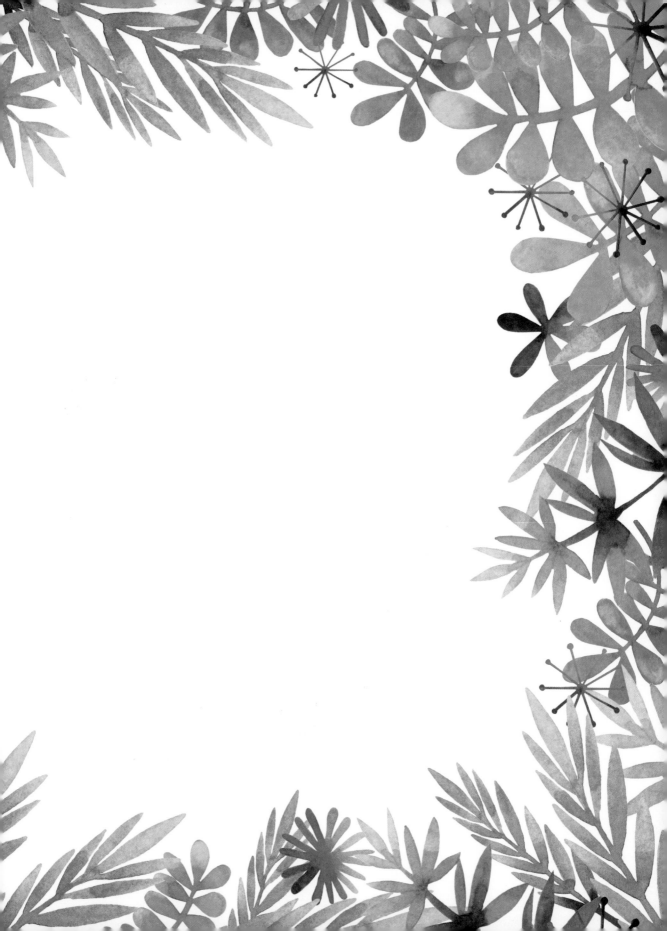

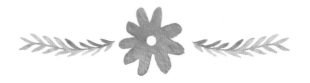

ONCE UPON A TIME

A single large capital acts as a decorative accent at the beginning of a body of text and invites the reader into the story. These letters were inspired by the traditional versals used in old manuscripts. Fill the letter shapes with any colour or pattern that suits the subject you are writing about. One decorated capital is enough to set the tone for each page of your magical memories. These letters can be written in different sizes using the same tools.

● TOOLS

- H pencil
- Coloured fine-line markers
- Soft white eraser

Alternative tools:
- Coloured pencils or gel pens

● LETTER-SPACING GUIDE

These capitals were designed for use as a single letter to accent the beginning of a body of text. Three spacing examples are shown here.

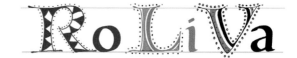

● DISTINGUISHING FEATURES

These large Uncial-style versals filled with colour and pattern produce decorative capitals for use as a visual entry point for a body of text. The large, round, outlined letters have long serifs with swollen ends. A variety of patterns and colours are demonstrated here, but letters can be filled with any colour or pattern you choose. A border of dots or scallops can be added to provide additional embellishment to the letters if desired.

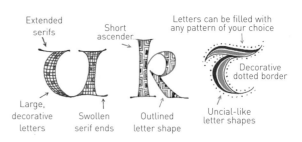

Extended serifs

Short ascender

Letters can be filled with any pattern of your choice

Decorative dotted border

Large, decorative letters

Swollen serif ends

Outlined letter shape

Uncial-like letter shapes

● LETTER CONSTRUCTION

1. Use an H pencil to sketch the letter outline.

2. Ink the outline with a fine-line marker, rotating the page whenever it is helpful. Add a little weight to the ends of the serifs.

3. Fill the letter with a pattern of your choice. Here, start with the vertical lines. Note how they are influenced by the letter shape.

4. Add the horizontal lines. Erase any noticeable pencil lines when the ink is dry, then add colour to random tiles.

● VARIATIONS

Alternative, more traditional capital letter forms for A, H and T filled with some new pattern ideas.

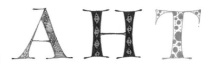

TIP

Use Roman Minuscules (pages 160–161) or Uncial (pages 190–191) as the lowercase letters and numbers for this alphabet.

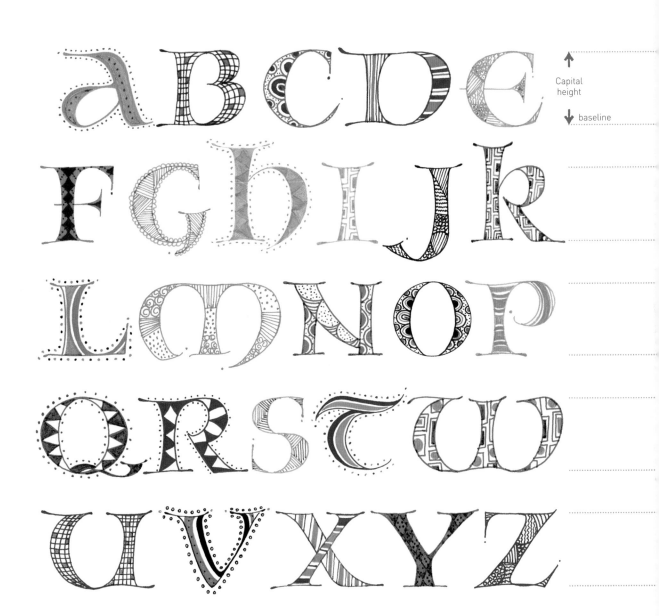

Capital height

baseline

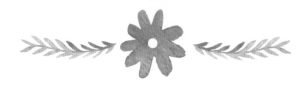

ABCDEFGHIJKLM

↑

Capital
height

↓ baseline

NOPQRSTUVWXYZ

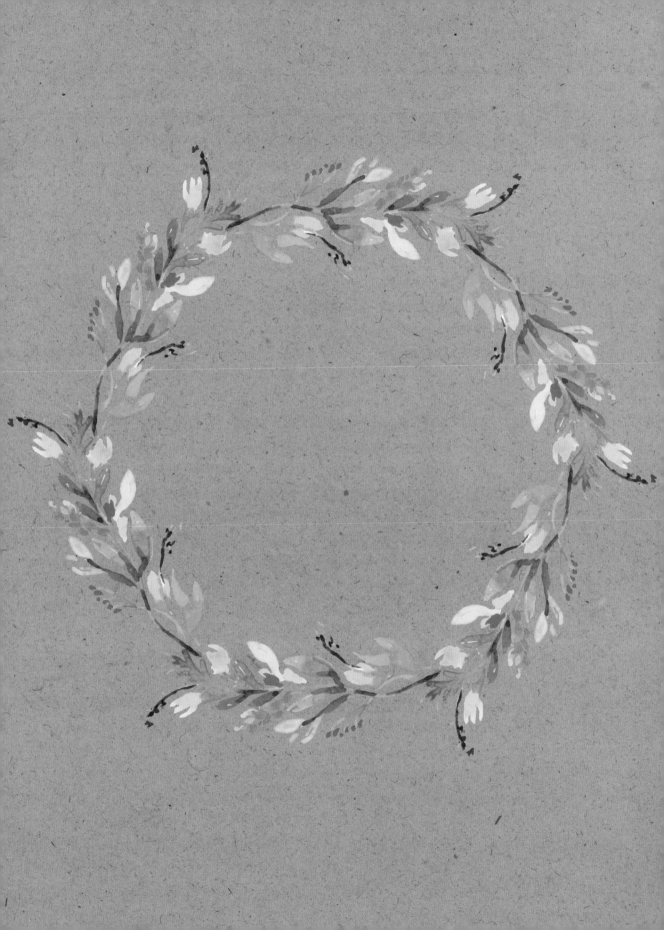

MADELINE

This is a lighthearted and versatile alphabet with a casual feel. It is easy to learn and fun to write, and can be drawn with any monoline tool. This letter style can be used to record everyday fun, birthday parties or pet adventures. Text can be adapted to your page by tucking in a smaller letter here and there, or by extending a kick-leg at the end of a line. To adjust the size of this alphabet, simply use finer- or heavier-weight writing tools.

TOOLS

- 0.70 mm pigmented fine-line marker

Alternative tools:
- Experiment to see what weights and colours are most appropriate for your project; try pencils, markers or gel pens.

LETTER-SPACING GUIDE

Letters dance up and down on the baseline, and some reach beyond the guidelines. The size of the o is varied to ease spacing and add visual interest.

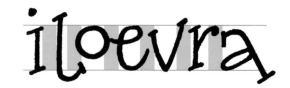

DISTINGUISHING FEATURES

This cheerful alphabet has low-branching letters, angular bowls and a round o. Vertical strokes begin and end with casually drawn serifs. An alternate o size (shown in the letter-spacing guide above right) and inconsistent serif angles allow you to improvise as you write, so that the letters can be packed quite closely together. Pulling the right leg of the a, h, m, n and k at the end of sentences or text lines gives the alphabet a casual feel.

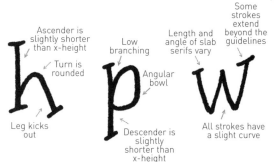

LETTER CONSTRUCTION

I. Beginning at the top, draw a vertical stroke.

2. Branch out the second stroke from within the first and curl around at the tip to create a ball.

3. Start the third stroke so that it overlaps the second without touching the first. Extend the stroke slightly beyond the baseline.

4. Add serifs of varying lengths and angles.

TIP

Use Madeline Capitals (pages 60–61) as the uppercase letters for this alphabet.

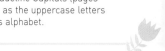

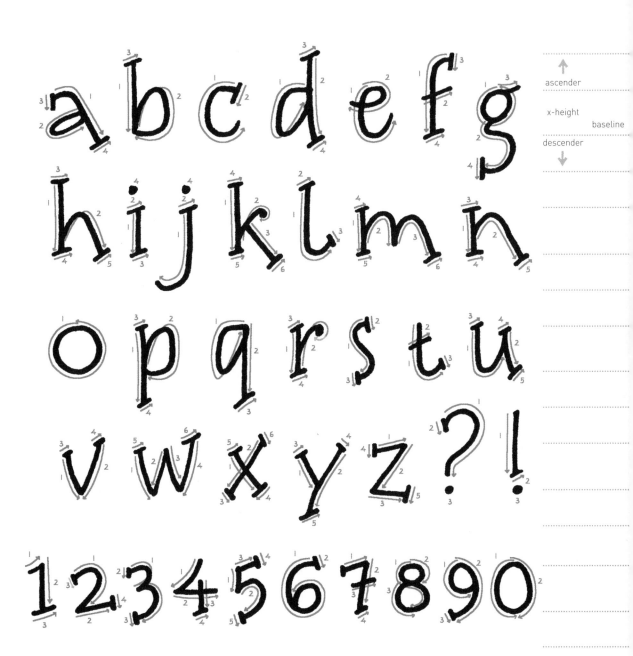

ascender

x-height

baseline

descender

MADELINE CAPITALS

This alphabet is primarily intended for use with the lowercase Madeline, but can also be employed alone for casual titles and short, cheerful captions about things such as cooking with Grandma or visiting with friends. The varied heights and widths of these letters give the impression that they are skipping across the page. Use a marker with a larger tip to create larger lettering or a smaller tip for a scaled-down version of this alphabet.

● TOOLS

- 0.70 mm pigmented fine-line marker

Alternative tools:
- Experiment to see what weights and colours are most appropriate for your project; try pencils, markers or gel pens.

● LETTER-SPACING GUIDE

Some letters reach beyond the guidelines.

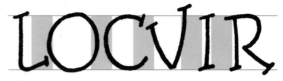

● DISTINGUISHING FEATURES

This modern monoline letter style has rounded bowls that may vary in size, and verticals that are not quite straight. The carefree serifs vary in length and are often drawn at different angles. Kick-legs can be extended to fill space at the end of a line or pulled below the baseline for tighter spacing. Letters are allowed to slant slightly forward and backward to help give the alphabet a feeling of movement.

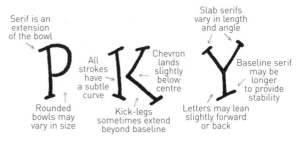

Serif is an extension of the bowl

Rounded bowls may vary in size

All strokes have a subtle curve

Kick-legs sometimes extend beyond baseline

Chevron lands slightly below centre

Slab serifs vary in length and angle

Baseline serif may be longer to provide stability

Letters may lean slightly forward or back

● LETTER CONSTRUCTION

1. Draw a vertical stroke, beginning at the top. Note that all strokes have a subtle curve to them.

2. Start the second stroke so that it overlaps the first and is slightly curved.

3. Draw the third stroke so that it ends by overlapping the second stroke.

4. Add slab serifs of varying lengths and angles.

TIP

Use Madeline (pages 58–59) as the lowercase letters and numbers for this alphabet.

A B C D E F

Capital height

baseline

G H I J K L

M N O P Q

R S T U V

W X Y Z

A B C D E F G H I J K L M N

↑
Capital
height

↓ baseline

a b c d e f g h i j k l m

↑
ascender

x-height
baseline

descender
↓

O P Q R S T U V W X Y Z

n o p q r s t u v w x y z

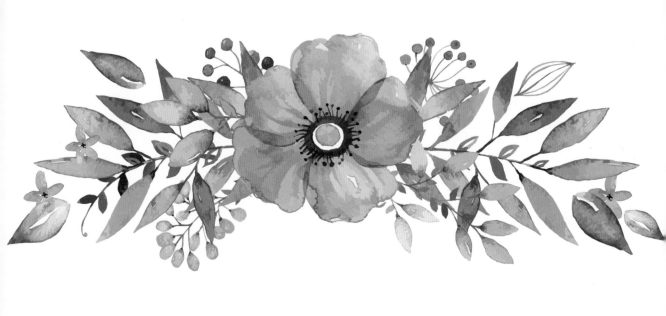
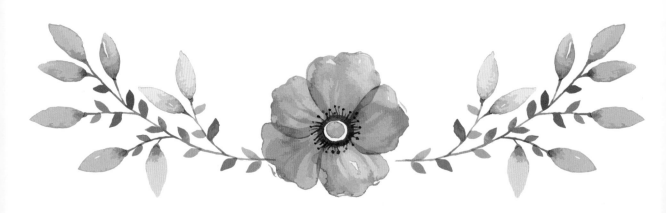

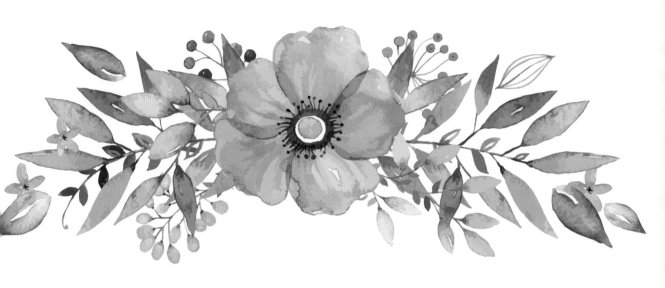

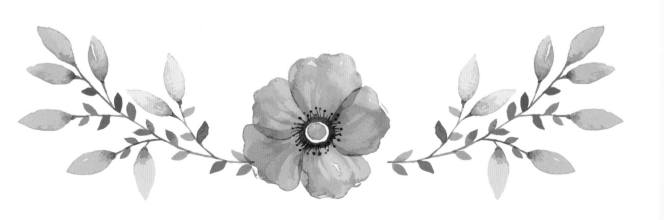

CLEOPATRA

These unique and unusual letters include shapes that are reminiscent of ancient Egypt. Serendipitously, they also look like the paper clips you might use to hold treasured travel memorabilia together until it can be added to a scrapbook. This alphabet is a pleasure to use and adds interest to pages about foreign lands and historical tours. Larger titles can be written using the same monoline tool, but a finer tool should be used for smaller text.

TOOLS

- Medium-point permanent marker

Alternative tools:
- Any monoline writing tool

LETTER-SPACING GUIDE

Make some letters shorter and tuck them under the arms of diagonal letters (v, w, y). Descenders drop below the baseline.

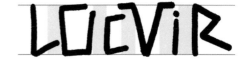

DISTINGUISHING FEATURES

This is a monocase alphabet created with a monoline tool, consisting of vertical letters constructed from simple geometric shapes. The triangular peaks and valleys used for some letters are reminiscent of the pyramids and are also found in Egyptian hieroglyphics. Other letters have trapezoid bowls that look like rectangular paper clips and are similar to the decorative elements found on the rims of ancient artefacts. There are no serifs on the letters, although V, W, X and Y do have short horizontal entry and exit strokes. Some letters have very short ascenders or descenders.

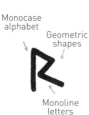
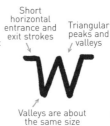
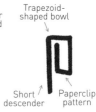

Monocase alphabet

Geometric shapes

Monoline letters

Short horizontal entrance and exit strokes

Triangular peaks and valleys

Valleys are about the same size

Trapezoid-shaped bowl

Short descender

Paperclip pattern

LETTER CONSTRUCTION

1. Draw the core shape without any pen lifts. Pause before each direction change.

2. Begin the second stroke above mid-height. Notice that there are no parallel lines.

3. Start the third stroke so that it overlaps the second and drops to just below mid-height.

TIP

This is a monocase alphabet without separate upper- and lowercase letters.

Capital height

baseline

A B C D E F G

H I J K L M N O

P Q R S T U V

W X Y Z ? ! 1 2

3 4 5 6 7 8 9 0

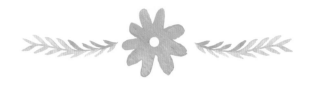

a b c d e f g h i j k l m n

o p q r s t u v w x y z

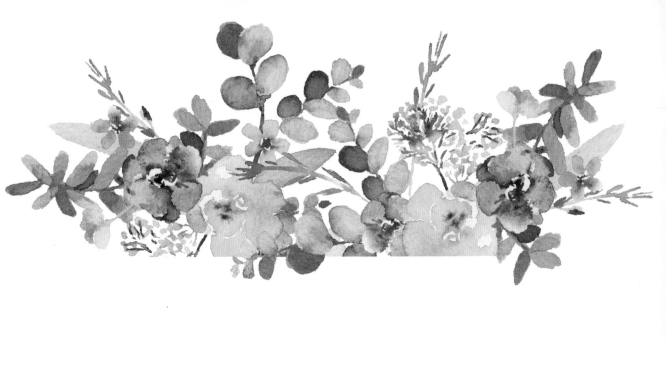
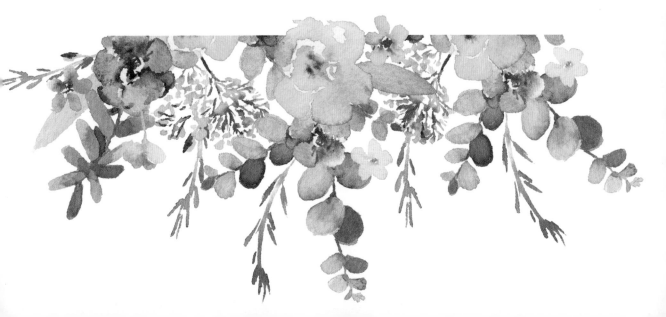

ART DECO

Traditional round letters can be given an Art Deco appearance when a substantial contrast in line weights is used. This alphabet has the feel of high society during the roaring twenties. Use this letter style for labels and text about old black-and-white photos of Grandma, classic cars or special outings to the theatre to give your pages the jazzy, upscale feel of Broadway. To adjust the size of the alphabet, use finer- or heavier-weight markers.

TOOLS

- 0.50 mm pigmented fine-line marker
- 5.0 mm pigmented calligraphy marker

Alternative tools:
- Traditional broad-edged dip pen and calligraphy fountain pen

LETTER-SPACING GUIDE

All letters sit on the baseline.

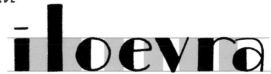

DISTINGUISHING FEATURES

The bold vertical strokes are made with a calligraphy marker at an x-height of just over 2 nib widths and are complemented by horizontal lines and round bowls that are carefully drawn with a fine-line marker. These letters sit comfortably on the baseline and have round bowls of consistent size that break into the guidelines. Portions of a, c, e, g and o require shading equal in width to the calligraphic tip. The top-left corners of some diagonal strokes also need to be drawn and filled in. Ascenders and descenders are equal to the x-height.

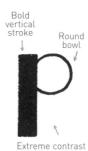
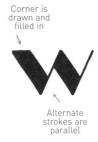

Thin horizontal stroke

Widest part of filled-in area equals 1 nib width

Bold vertical stroke

Round bowl

Corner is drawn and filled in

Extreme contrast in line weight

Alternate strokes are parallel

LETTER CONSTRUCTION

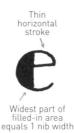

I. Using a fine-line marker, make the top of the first stroke almost flat.

2. Draw an oval bowl about three-quarters of the x-height. Let it overlap and extend slightly beyond the first stroke.

3. Use a calligraphy marker to measure the width of the shaded area, allowing the nib to overlap the bowl outline.

4. Use the fine-line marker to fill in the shaded area.

TIP

Use Art Deco Capitals (pages
76–77) as the uppercase letters
for this alphabet.

☐ 0° dominant pen angle (all other angles are indicated next to the stroke)

2 + nib
widths

2 + nib
widths

2 + nib
widths

ascender

x-height

baseline

descender

a b c d e f g

h i j k l m n

o p q r s t u

v w x y z ! ?

1 2 3 4 5 6 7 8 9 0

⬛ Indicates area that requires shading (see Letter Construction guidelines, opposite)

ART DECO CAPITALS

This Art Deco-inspired alphabet can be used alone for titles and short captions, or with the lowercase Art Deco for longer pieces of text. These stylized letters have big impact and need to be written slowly and carefully to ensure a slick, look. Use finer- or heavier-weight tools to create the letters in different sizes. Some letters require shading, and the corners of the diagonal letters need to be drawn and filled in.

TOOLS

- 5.0 mm pigmented calligraphy marker
- 0.50 mm pigmented fine-line marker

Alternative tools:
- Traditional broad-edged dip pen and calligraphy fountain pen

LETTER-SPACING GUIDE

All letters sit on the baseline. Each letter acts as a block or unit. The units are placed side by side, with the exception of I, which should be given the same unit space as L.

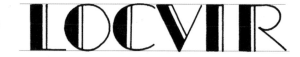

DISTINGUISHING FEATURES

These very consistent block letters line up carefully along the baseline. Wide vertical strokes are accented with contrasting fine lines and large, round bowls. Notice the elegant high-waisting and the gentle upward curve in the K and the bowls of B, P and R. Also note the short lines that connect the fine strokes to the wide ones. The heavy verticals are drawn 4 nib-widths high with a flat pen angle. Allow the gentle curve of round letters and the valley points of the W to break the baseline.

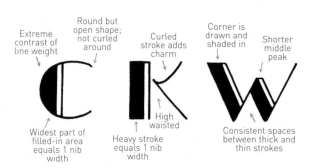

Extreme contrast of line weight

Round but open shape; not curled around

Widest part of filled-in area equals 1 nib width

Curled stroke adds charm

Heavy stroke equals 1 nib width

High waisted

Corner is drawn and shaded in

Shorter middle peak

Consistent spaces between thick and thin strokes

LETTER CONSTRUCTION

1. Using a calligraphy marker at a 50° pen angle, pull the first downward stroke.

2. Use a fine-line marker to extend the second stroke upward from the angle at the bottom of the first stroke.

3. Use the fine-line marker to add a thin line parallel to the heavy stroke, then draw the corner and connecting stroke.

4. Fill in the corner shading with the fine-line marker.

TIP

Use Art Deco (pages 74–75) as the lowercase letters and numbers for this alphabet.

0° dominant pen angle (all other angles are indicated next to the stroke)

4 nib widths

Capital height

baseline

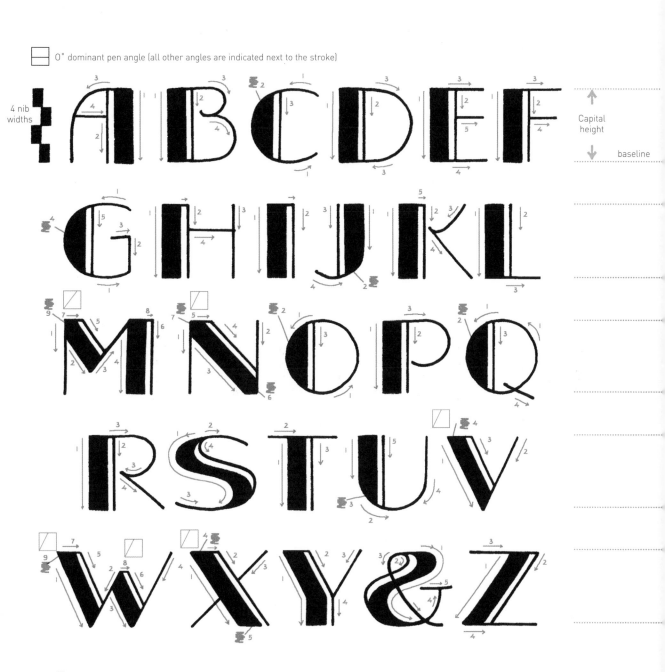

Indicates area that requires shading (see Letter Construction guidelines, opposite)

A B C D E F G H I J K L M N

↑

Capital
height

↓ baseline

a b c d e f g h i j k l m

↑
ascender

x-height

baseline

descender
↓

OPQRSTUVWXY&Z

nopqrstuvwxyz

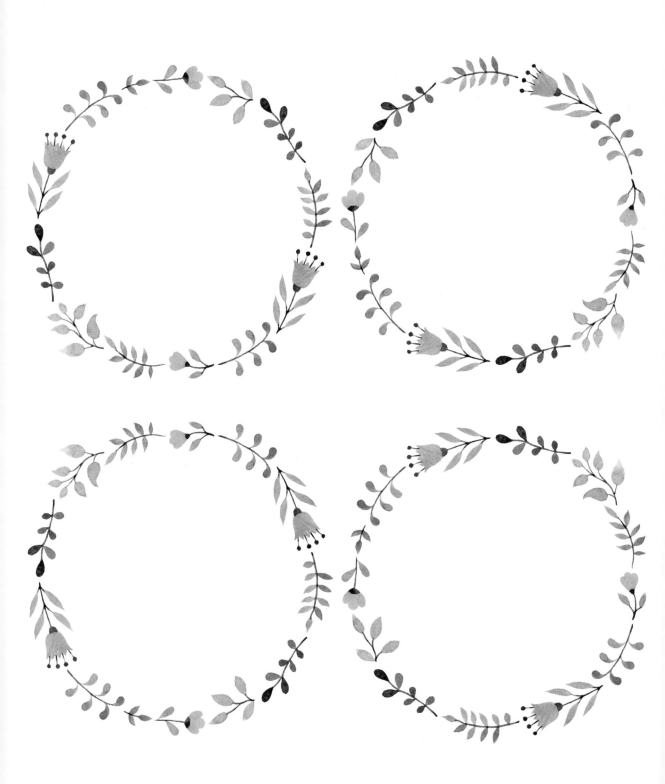

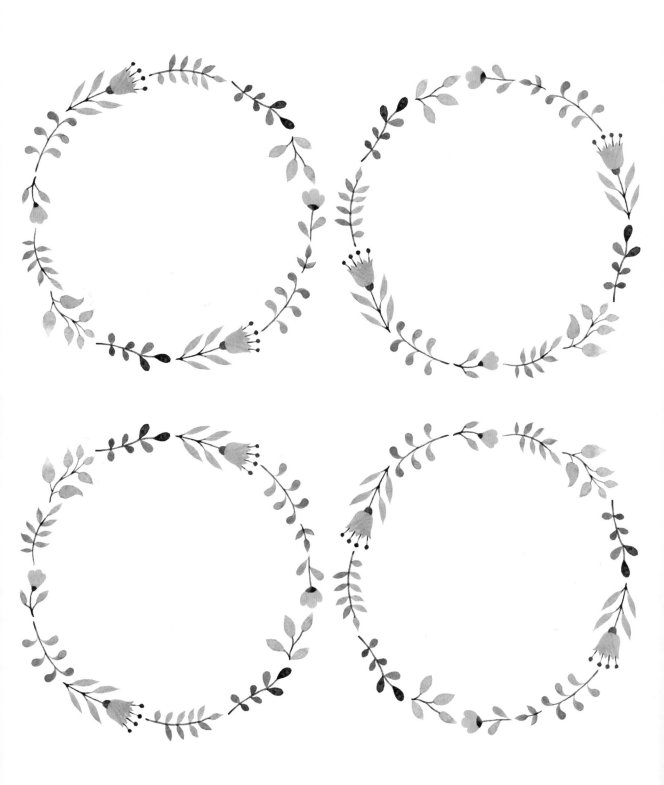

EASTERN BAZAAR

This alphabet's Asian flavour comes from the tapered strokes and the use of a brush marker. The letter strokes are created using pressure and quick release, which may require some practice. Intended for titles and captions only, this letter style is perfect for recording memories of once-in-a-lifetime holidays or for a special event featuring your favourite take-away food. Try fibre brushes in a variety of sizes for lettering at different heights.

● TOOLS

- Pigmented fibre-tipped brush marker with 10-mm (⅜-inch) long tapered tip

Alternative tools:
- Pointed brush pen

● LETTER-SPACING GUIDE

The tips of the letters cut through the guidelines.

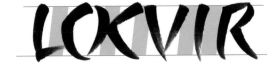

● DISTINGUISHING FEATURES

Unusual letter shapes are constructed from a series of tapered strokes. These often end in slightly textured or wispy points that break through the guidelines. Letters have flat tops and often include short strokes that are made by releasing the pressure on the brush with a quick flick. This alphabet has a slight forward slant, but strokes within the same letter can have a slightly different tilt.

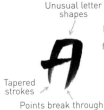

Unusual letter shapes

Letters slant forward

Flat-topped bowl

Centre stroke tapers to the left

Tapered strokes

Points break through the guidelines

Short strokes made with a quick flick

Upward lift on bottom stroke

● LETTER CONSTRUCTION

1. Position the brush marker as shown for each stroke. Apply pressure and then pull the first stroke downward. Note the stroke's slight curve and slant.

2. Apply pressure, then use a quick flick and release of pressure to taper the second stroke.

3. Begin the third stroke, quickly adding and then releasing pressure to taper it at both ends.

4. Apply pressure then pull the fourth stroke downward, releasing the pressure gradually to taper the stroke.

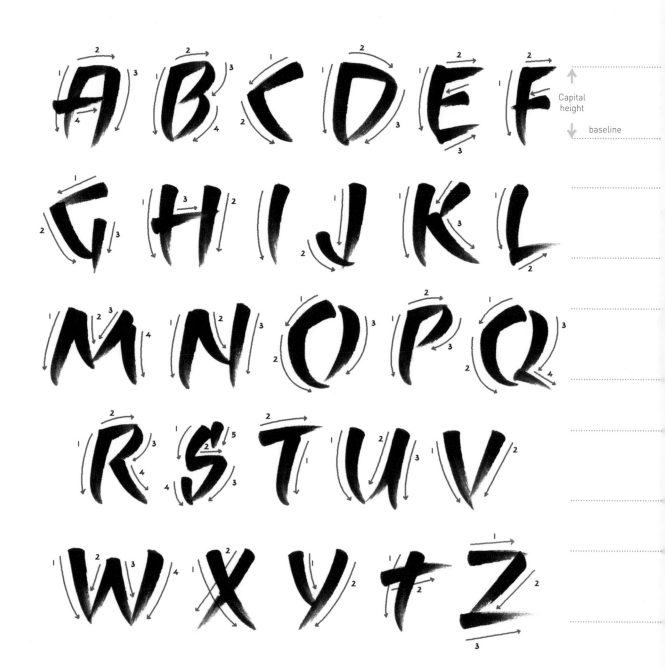

Capital height

baseline

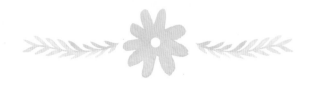

A B C D E F G H I J K L M N

↑
Capital
height

↓   baseline

O P Q R S T U V W X Y t Z

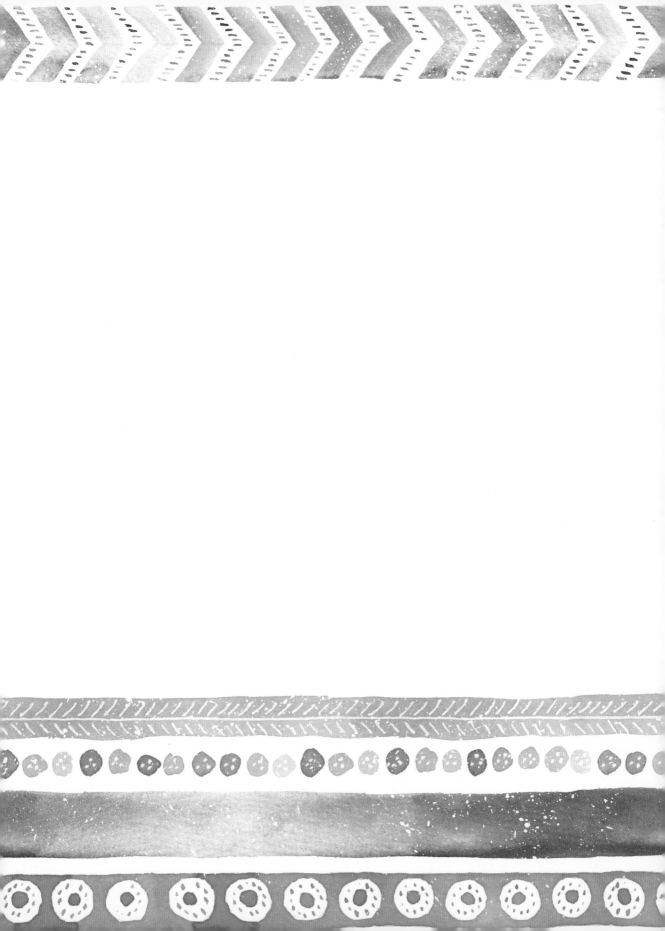

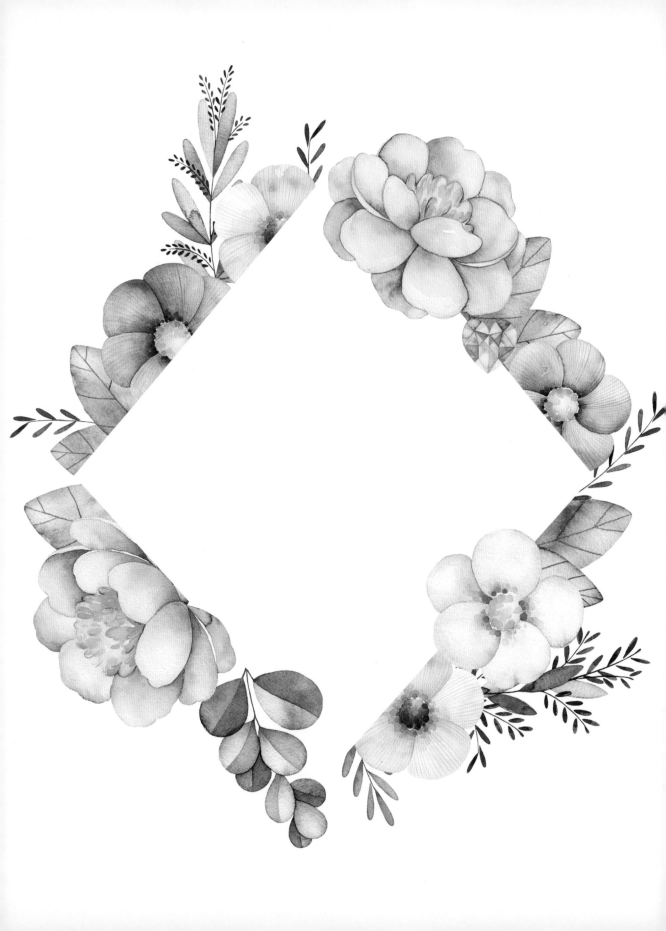

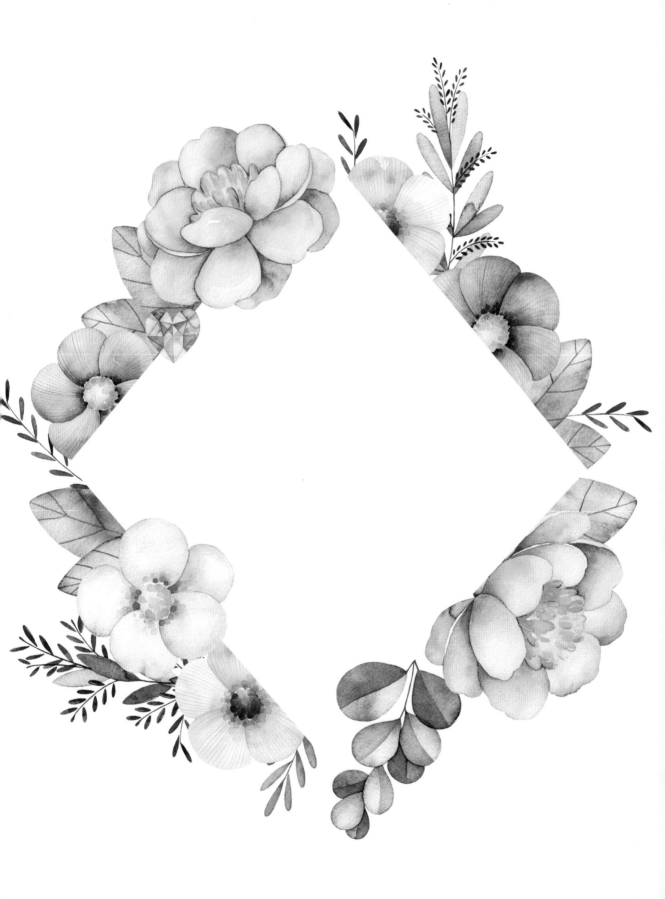

CURLS

Curls in all the right places give these carefully drawn, dancing letters a touch of whimsy. Use this letter style any time you have an upbeat but informal event to remember, such as an afternoon tea party, or use it for a bridal shower invitation. This alphabet can be written in a variety of sizes using the same tools, and you can mix and match pencil colours.

TOOLS

- Coloured pencils

Alternative tools:
- Fine-line markers or gel pens

LETTER-SPACING GUIDE

Letters lean forward and back. Some letters extend beyond the guidelines.

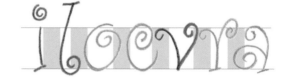

DISTINGUISHING FEATURES

Curls is a monoline alphabet with no straight lines. Tilting the letters forward and backward while they remain on the baseline creates a feeling of movement. Mid x-height branching letters have oval bowls that are fairly consistent in size and shape, and often burst through the guidelines. Larger curls are included where they will not interfere with letter spacing, and smaller curls are added to the letter stems. Ascenders and descenders are slightly shorter than the x-height, and most verticals have a single bottom serif for stability.

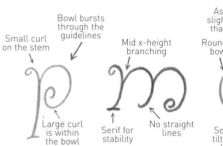

LETTER CONSTRUCTION

I. Begin the first stroke just below the top guideline and curl around.

2. Start the second stroke so that it overlaps the first. The bowl is just over half the x-height and extends left.

3. Add a short serif to the bottom of the first stroke. Note that the serif is not parallel to the baseline.

TIP

You can find the uppercase letters for this alphabet in Curls Capitals on pages 92–93.

ascender

x-height

baseline

descender

a b c d e f g

h i j k l m n

o p q r s t u

v w x y z ? !

1 2 3 4 5 6 7 8 9 0

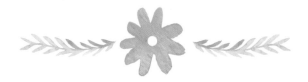

CURLS CAPITALS

Designed for use with the lowercase Curls letters, these capitals add a touch of class to this whimsical alphabet. It is perfect for creating invitations or recording social events such as garden parties, baby showers or a teddy bears' picnic. These letters can easily be adapted to a variety of sizes without even changing your writing tool. All you have to do is alter the pencil colour to suit the event or to match your invitation.

● TOOLS

- Coloured pencils

Alternative tools:
- Fine-line markers or gel pens

● LETTER-SPACING GUIDE

This uppercase alphabet was designed for use only with the lowercase letters, not to be used alone. These three spacing examples demonstrate some upper- and lowercase letters together.

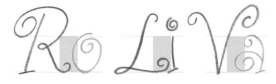

● DISTINGUISHING FEATURES

Curls Capitals is written slowly and carefully using coloured pencils. All letters sit on the baseline, although large oval bowls break through the guidelines slightly. Larger curls act as flourishes, while smaller curls and serifs are added to the letter stems to provide balance and stability. Notice that all the lines in this alphabet have a slight curve to them. Although this alphabet was written at a 30° slant, the slant should be varied when used with the lowercase letters.

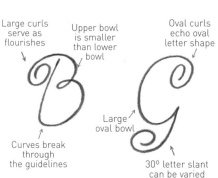

Large curls serve as flourishes

Upper bowl is smaller than lower bowl

Curves break through the guidelines

Large oval bowl

30° letter slant can be varied when combined with lowercase letters

Oval curls echo oval letter shape

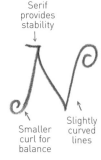

Serif provides stability

Smaller curl for balance

Slightly curved lines

● LETTER CONSTRUCTION

1. Begin the first stroke just below the guideline and curl around. Notice the slight curve in the downstroke.

2. Starting the second stroke within the first, branch up and around to make a large curl.

3. Start the third crossbar stroke with a tight curl and then cross the first stroke at about mid-height.

4. Add a serif to the bottom of the first stroke for stability.

TIP

Use Curls (pages 90–91) as the lowercase letters and numbers for this alphabet.

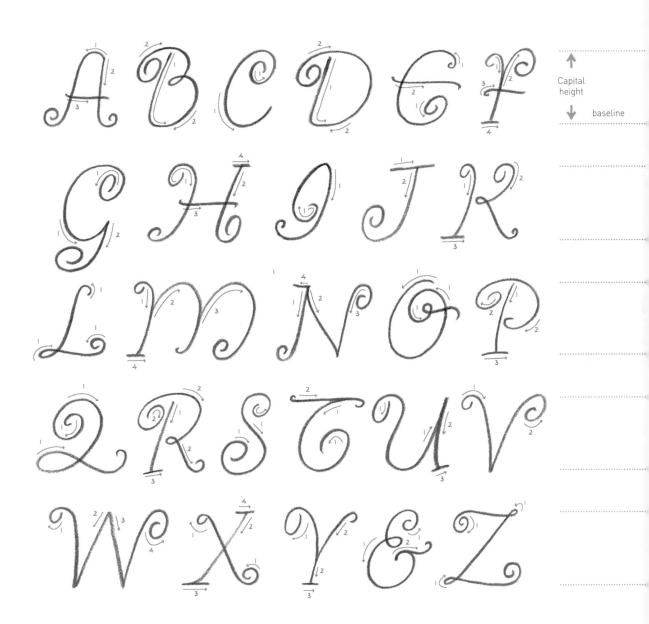

Capital height

baseline

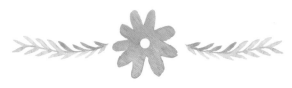

A B C D E F G H I J K L M N

↑
Capital
height

↓ baseline

a b c d e f g h i j k l m

↑
ascender

x-height

baseline

descender
↓

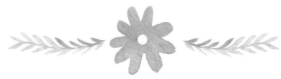

O P Q R S T U V W X Y & Z

n o p q r s t u v w x y z

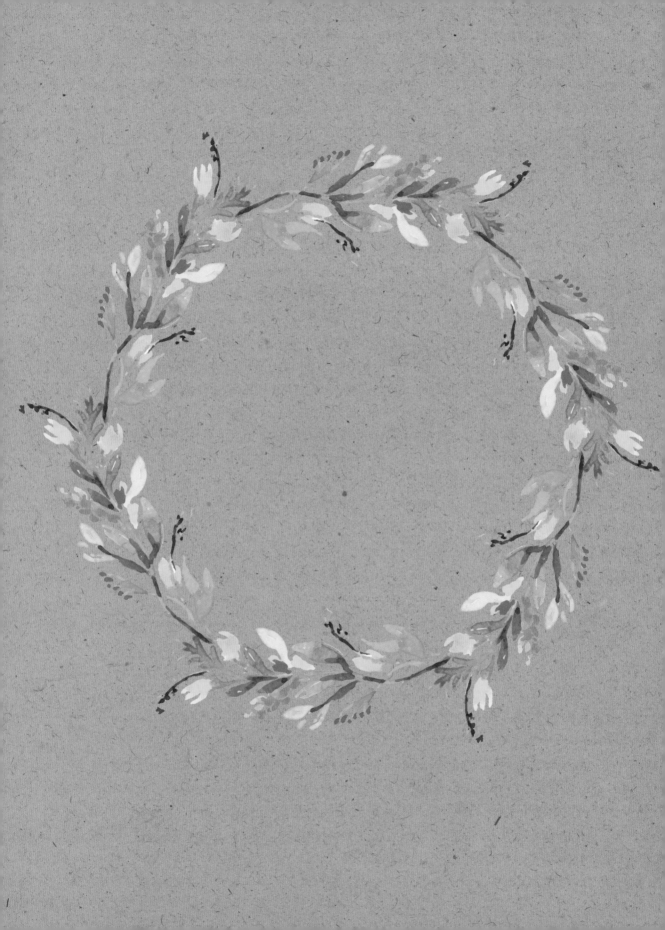

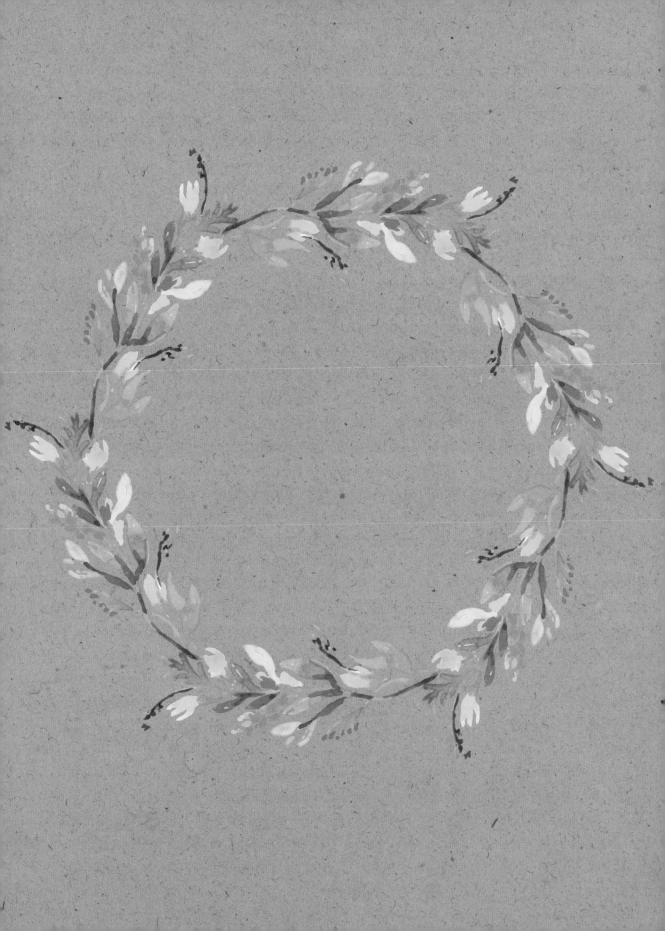

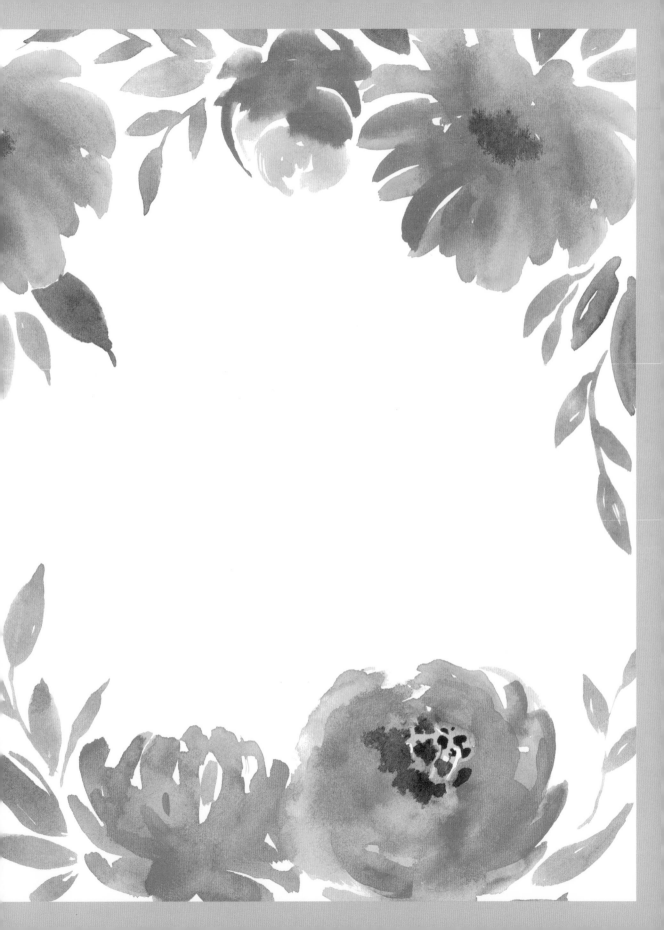

SHOP FRONT

You might find lettering like this in shop windows or on signs announcing 'Daily Specials' on your many travels. This is an excellent alphabet for captions or titles about the marvels of daytrippers and globetrotters alike. The tool used to create this alphabet may be a little unfamiliar, but with some practice it is fun to use. Pay careful attention to the start and finish of each stroke. Use a different-sized brush marker for larger or smaller lettering.

TOOLS

- Pigmented fibre-tipped brush marker with 13-mm (½-inch) long tapered tip

Alternative tools:
- Coloured fibre-tipped brush markers

LETTER-SPACING GUIDE

All letters sit on the baseline.

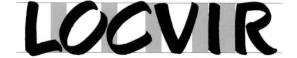

DISTINGUISHING FEATURES

This bold alphabet is written with a flexible fibre-tipped brush marker, which requires practice to master. The sans-serif letters are fairly consistent in weight, size and shape, and a jaunty disposition is achieved by giving each stroke a slight curve. Bowls are forward-slanting oval shapes. A range of interlinear spacing is possible with this letter style, but it is most effective if the lines of text are no more than one x-height apart.

All strokes have a slight curve to them

Small gap

Be conscious of how each stroke begins and ends

Chevron at mid x-height

Bold sans-serif strokes

Forward-slanted oval bowl

Letters are vertical

LETTER CONSTRUCTION

1. Position the brush marker as shown. Apply pressure and then pull the brush downward at a slight slant. Note that all the strokes have a slight curve.

2. Turning the brush slightly as shown, place the tip so that it overlaps the first stroke, then apply pressure before pulling the second stroke.

3. Repeat this process for the third stroke. Make sure that you come to a complete stop before lifting the brush.

4. Make the fourth stroke as before. Notice that alternate strokes have a similar slant.

TIP

Shop Front is intended for titles and captions only. Use Miss Barrett (pages 128–129) at a smaller size for accompanying pieces of long text.

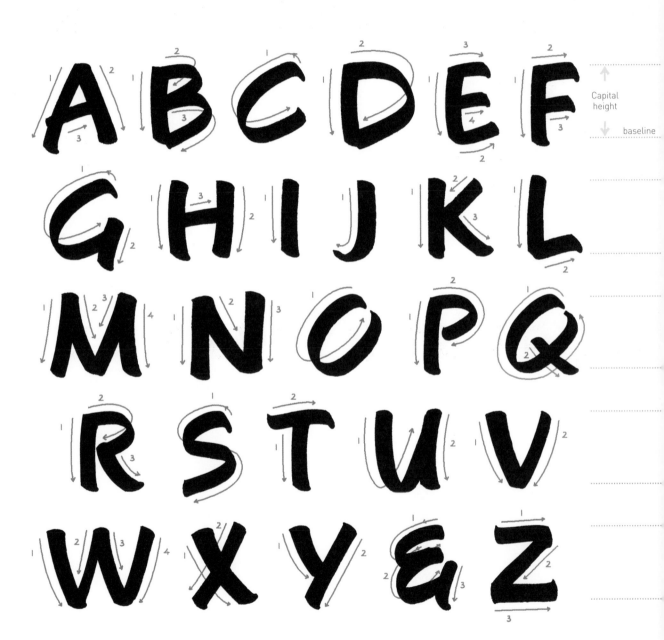

Capital
height

baseline

A B C D E F G H I J K L M N

Capital
height

baseline

O P Q R S T U V W X Y & Z

STICK LETTERS

This lighthearted alphabet is fun and easy to draw. It is created using the end of a modified lolly stick to stamp the letter strokes. Use a larger or smaller stick to create the letters in different sizes. There is no need to make perfect letters – you can line them up and space them neatly, or allow them to stumble across your page. This alphabet is great for captioning photo albums of adventure holidays in the great outdoors.

● TOOLS

- Modified lolly stick
- Ink pad
- Pigmented marker with tip equal to stick width

● LETTER-SPACING GUIDE

All letters can sit on the baseline as shown, or they can tumble and skip along it.

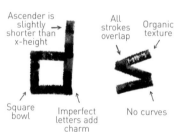

● DISTINGUISHING FEATURES

The letters are constructed from a series of stamped shapes. Organic-looking strokes overlap each other to create square bowls and add stability. This process often results in imperfect letters, but this just adds to the alphabet's charm. Longer strokes require an extra overlapping stamp, while some of the numbers have shorter sections that need to be drawn in with a marker. Ascenders and descenders are slightly shorter than the x-height.

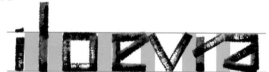

Ascender is slightly shorter than x-height →

All strokes overlap

Organic texture

Longer strokes require multiple stamps ↓

↑ Square bowl

↑ Imperfect letters add charm

No curves

Counter spaces are about equal width

● LETTER CONSTRUCTION

1. Press the stick onto the ink pad, then stamp the first stroke on a diagonal.

2. Stamp the second stroke so that it overlaps the first. Apply more ink to the stick whenever required.

3. Apply a third stamp to extend the second stroke and form the descender.

4. Stamp a final stroke that overlaps the second stroke and extends it to the top of the x-height.

TIP

Use Stick Letter Capitals (pages 106–107) as the uppercase letters for this alphabet.

a b c d e f g

ascender

x-height

baseline

descender

h i j k l m n o

p q r s t u v

w x y z ! ? o l

2 3 4 5 6 7 8 9

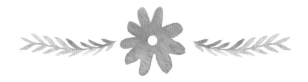

STICK LETTER CAPITALS

These wacky, built-up letters look like campfire kindling. Each letter is created using the sanded end of a wooden stick to stamp multiple strokes. A larger lolly stick is used here, because it produces longer strokes than that used to create the coordinating lowercase alphabet. Use these laidback letters to record fireside stories, fishy tales or memories of hiking holidays.

⬤ TOOLS

- Large lolly stick
- Ink pad
- Pigmented marker with tip equal to stick width

⬤ LETTER-SPACING GUIDE

All letters can sit on the baseline as shown, or they can tumble and skip along it.

⬤ DISTINGUISHING FEATURES

Stamped strokes overlap and lean on one another to create these letters. Imperfect, straight-sided shapes and triangular bowls give this alphabet its rustic look. Each stamp leaves its own organic-looking texture. Multiple stamps are required to make substantial letters, and the tongue of the Q needs to be drawn in with a marker.

Organic texture →

Multiple stamps give weight to the stroke ↑

Stamped lines overlap and lean →

No curves ↑

Imperfect letters add to the natural look

Triangular bowls ↑

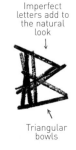

⬤ LETTER CONSTRUCTION

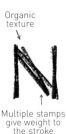

I. Press the stick onto the ink pad, then stamp the first vertical stroke. Apply more ink to the stick whenever required.

2. Place the second stroke on an angle and allow about a quarter of its length to overhang the first stroke.

3. Complete the triangular bowl with the third stroke, allowing it to overhang the first stroke.

4. Stamp three or four more strokes to give weight to the letter. Notice that they cross and lean on each other.

TIP

Use Stick Letters (pages 104–105) as the lowercase letters and numbers for this alphabet.

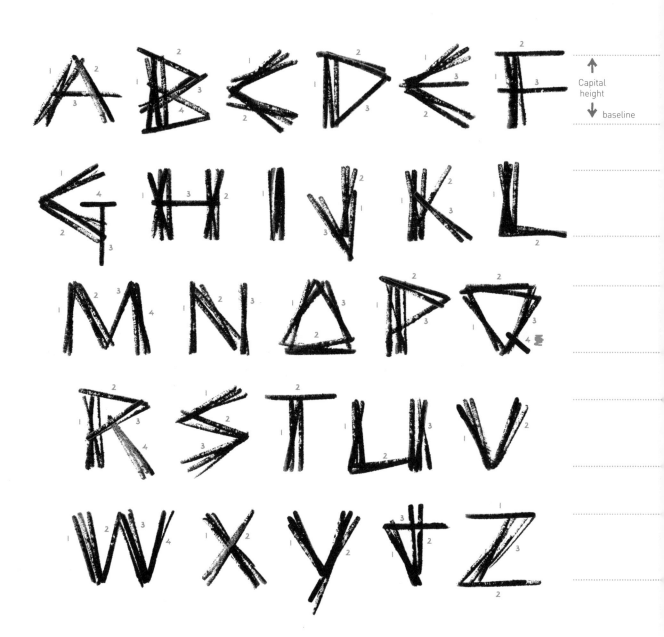

↑ Capital height

↓ baseline

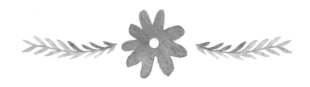

ABCDEFGHIJKLMN

↑
Capital
height

↓ baseline

abcdefghijklm

↑
ascender

x-height
baseline

descender
↓

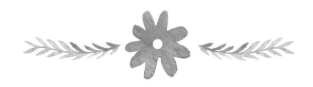

O P Q R S T U V W X Y Z

n o p q r s t u v w x y z

TROY

Inspired by ancient Greek symbols, this is an intriguing monocase alphabet that is fun to use. It is ideal for holiday stories about historical discoveries and ancient civilizations, or endless days on islands of boundless beauty. This letter style requires little practice and is created using everyday tools. It can be written at a wide variety of sizes using the same monoline tool, but a finer marker or pen should be used for very small lettering.

TOOLS

- Medium-point permanent marker

Alternative tools:
- Any monoline writing tool

LETTER-SPACING GUIDE

All letters sit on the baseline.

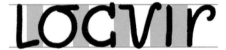

DISTINGUISHING FEATURES

The many round letters give this alphabet its warm, encompassing feel, while the heavy influence of Greek symbols creates an exotic look. Unusual monoline letter shapes include a top-heavy S, while the C, G, M, N, U and W shapes are based on the familiar omega symbol. Round letters have no vertical strokes but do have at least one horizontal terminal to give stability. There are no ascenders and only a few modest descenders, allowing a wide choice of interlinear spacing.

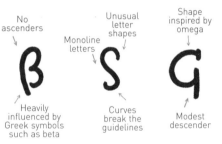

LETTER CONSTRUCTION

1. Beginning at the top, draw an S curve.

2. Draw the top bowl, starting and finishing it so that it overlaps the first stroke.

3. Draw the bottom bowl, again overlapping the first stroke at the beginning and end.

Capital height

baseline

α β C D E F G
H I J K L M N
O P Q R S T U
V W X Y Z ? !
1 2 3 4 5 6 7 8 9 0

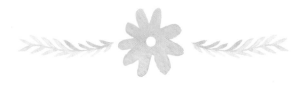

a β c d e f g h i j k l m

Capital height

baseline

n o p q r s t u v w x y z

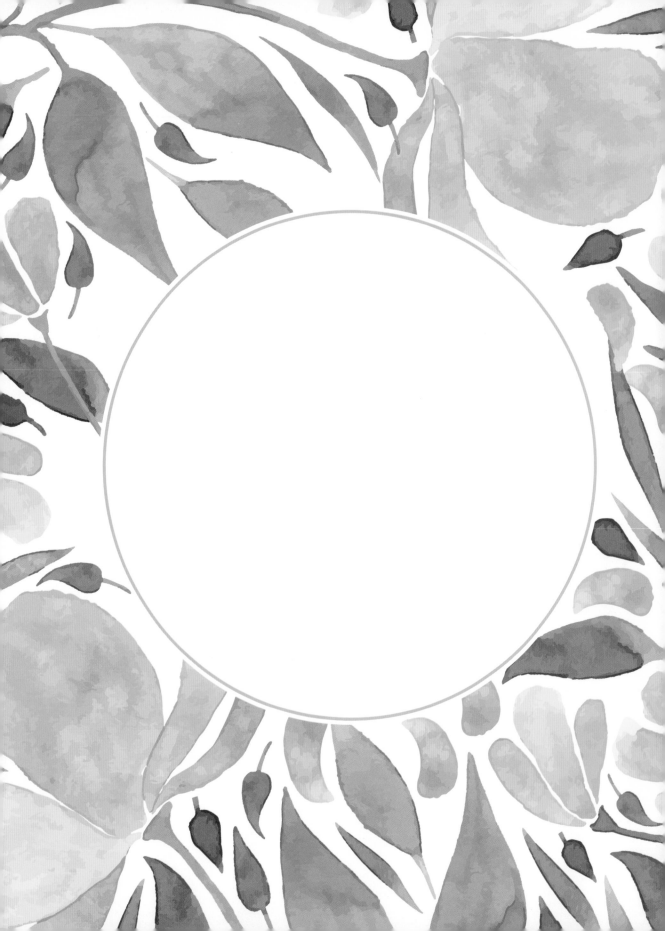

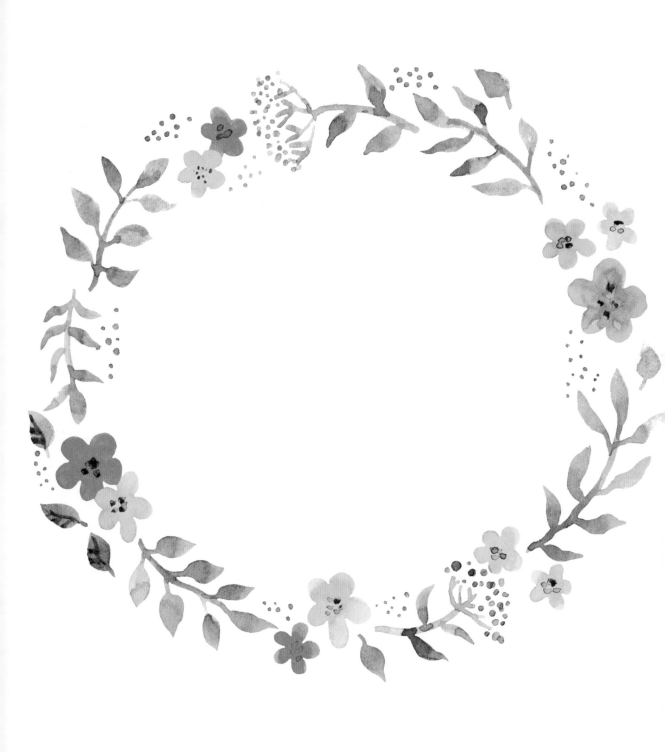

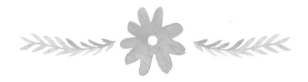

BRUSH EXPRESS

This lively and contemporary alphabet is great for high-energy title pages, and is especially appropriate for captions and phrases about teen parties and special events. The challenges of using a brush pen are well worth the effort, but special care should be taken to maintain fairly consistent letter weight within a project because minor changes in pressure will result in heavier- or lighter-weight letters. A range of letter sizes can be made with the same tool.

TOOLS

- Pointed brush pen

Wet and dry brushwork:
- Experiment with the brush to see the range of letter sizes that can be made.

LETTER-SPACING GUIDE

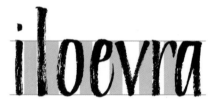

All letters sit on the baseline.

DISTINGUISHING FEATURES

These upright letters branch at mid x-height, and have ascenders and descenders that are slightly shorter than the x-height. They have angular bowls and somewhat narrow counter spaces. Contrasting thick and thin strokes are achieved by varying the pressure on the brush. Textured strokes are achieved by using a fairly dry brush on slightly rough paper. The texture adds to the dynamic appearance of this alphabet.

Ascender is slightly shorter than x-height

Mid x-height branching

Contrasting thick and thin strokes

Narrow, angular counter space

Textured strokes

Descender is slightly shorter than x-height

Vertical letters

Tapered stroke

LETTER CONSTRUCTION

1. Push the brush to the left before applying pressure on the downward stroke. Release the pressure and pull to the right to make a thin horizontal stroke. Apply pressure at the top of the second curve, then release slowly to taper.

2. Turn the brush anticlockwise slightly and apply pressure before pulling downward in a curved stroke.

3. Begin the third stroke with the same brush angle and pressure as the second stroke. Release the pressure quickly to taper the stroke.

TIP

Use Brush Express Capitals (pages 120–121) as the uppercase letters for this alphabet.

a b c d e f g

ascender

↑

x-height

↓ baseline

descender

h i j k l m n

o p q r s t u

v w x y z ? !

1 2 3 4 5 6 7 8 9 0

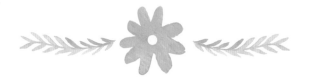

BRUSH EXPRESS CAPITALS

This spirited and modern alphabet is designed for use with the lowercase Brush Express letters or can be used alone for titles. It is appropriate for catchy headlines, noteworthy events and splashy title pages. Familiar letter shapes are given new life when made with a pointed brush pen. Although this tool may be challenging at first, a range of letter sizes and weights can be achieved by varying the amount of pressure applied to the brush.

TOOLS

- Pointed brush pen

Alternative tools:
- Experiment with the brush to see the range of letter sizes that can be made.

LETTER-SPACING GUIDE

All letters sit on the baseline.

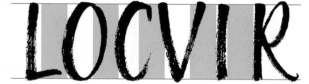

DISTINGUISHING FEATURES

These high-energy letters have verticals with a slight curve, horizontals that are not quite horizontal, and saucy brush flicks. Bowls that are either oval or angular and some hybrid shapes and widths contribute to the alphabet's contemporary feel. Contrasting thick and thin strokes are achieved by varying the pressure on the brush. This alphabet has an extreme textural quality due to the use of a moderately dry brush on a slightly rough surface.

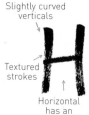

Slightly curved verticals

Oval bowl

Angular bowl

Textured strokes

Saucy brush flick

Horizontal has an upward tilt

Contrasting thick and thin strokes

Hybrid letter shapes

LETTER CONSTRUCTION

1. Position the brush as shown. Apply moderate pressure to draw the first stroke. Note the slant of the stroke.

2. Turn the brush slightly anticlockwise and apply pressure before pulling diagonally. Note the slight curve of the stroke.

3. Turn the brush clockwise and apply a little pressure for the third stroke. This stroke is a lighter weight than the two previous strokes.

4. Maintain the same brush angle but apply more pressure for a heavier-weight fourth stroke. Notice the slant of this stroke.

TIP

Use Brush Express (pages 118–119) as the lowercase letters and numbers for this alphabet.

A B C D E F

Capital height

baseline

G H I J K L

M N O P Q

R S T U V

W X Y & Z

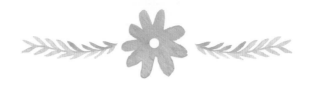

A B C D E F G H I J K L M N

Capital
height

↓ baseline

a b c d e f g h i j k l m

↑
ascender

x-height

baseline

descender
↓

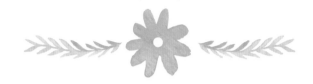

O P Q R S T U V W X Y & Z

n o p q r s t u v w x y z

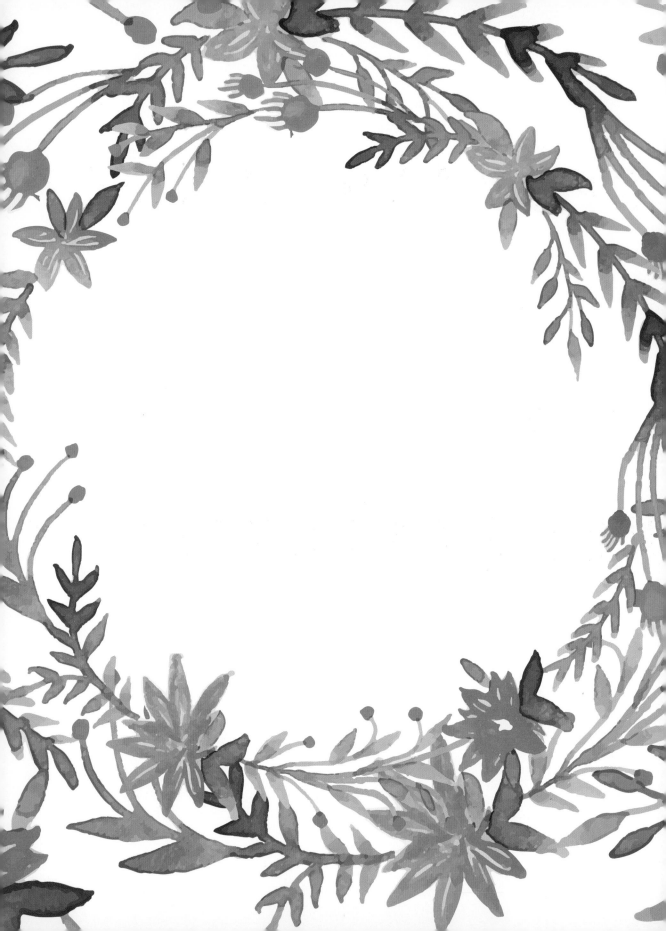

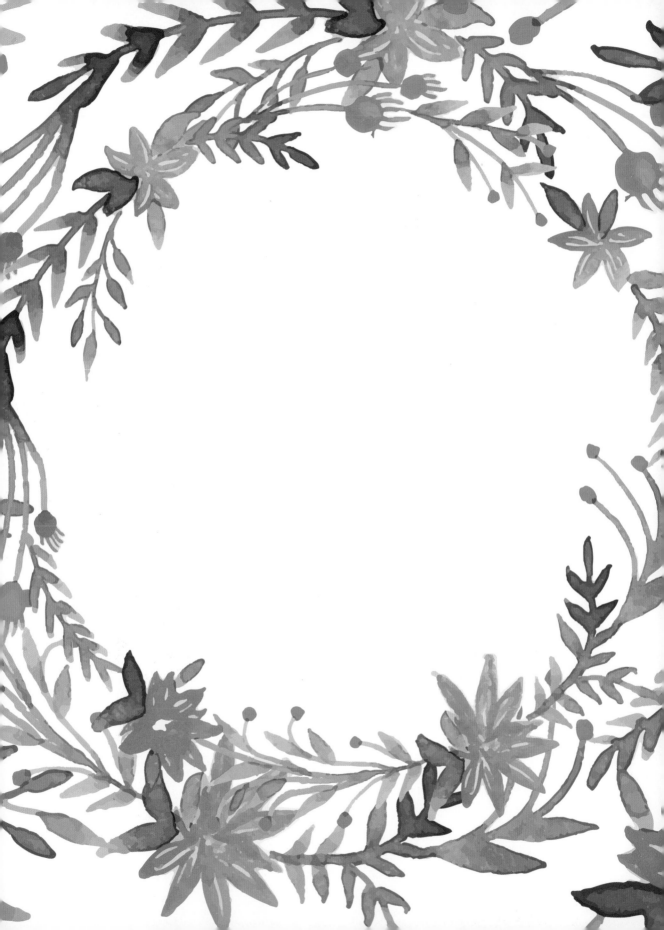

MISS BARRETT

This tidy printing has both warmth and understated class. It is appropriate for a wide variety of occasions, and can be used to record either short phrases or long bodies of text neatly. The letter shapes were inspired by Italic (pages 146–147), but are upright and written with a simple monoline tool. Use a larger tool when writing at larger sizes in order to maintain the same visual letter weight.

TOOLS

- 0.42 mm pigmented fine-line marker

Alternative tools:
- Use any monoline writing tool in any colour and size that suits your purpose.

LETTER-SPACING GUIDE

All letters sit on the baseline.

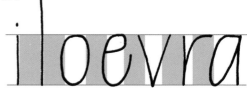

DISTINGUISHING FEATURES

These monoline letters are low branching and have oval bowls that are very consistent in size and shape. The ascenders and descenders are slightly shorter than the x-height, and the letters are vertical and without serifs. The natural imperfections that occur when the human hand uses a fine tool give this alphabet a sympathetic nature, while a sense of subtle refinement is suggested by the tall, slender, oval shape that is echoed throughout this style.

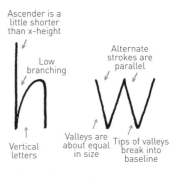

Ascender is a little shorter than x-height

Low branching

Vertical letters

Alternate strokes are parallel

Valleys are about equal in size

Tips of valleys break into baseline

Bowls are consistent in size and shape

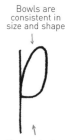

Descender is slightly shorter than x-height

LETTER CONSTRUCTION

1. Beginning at the top, draw a vertical stroke.

2. Briefly retrace the vertical before branching up and to the right.

3. Briefly retrace the second stroke before branching up and to the right. Notice that the counter spaces are about the same size.

TIP

Adapt Italic Capitals (pages 148–149) to use as uppercase letters for Miss Barrett.

a b c d e f g

ascender

x-height

baseline

descender

h i j k l m n

o p q r s t u v

w x y z ! ? 1 2

3 4 5 6 7 8 9 0

a b c d e f g h i j k l m

ascender

x-height

baseline

descender

n o p q r s t u v w x y z

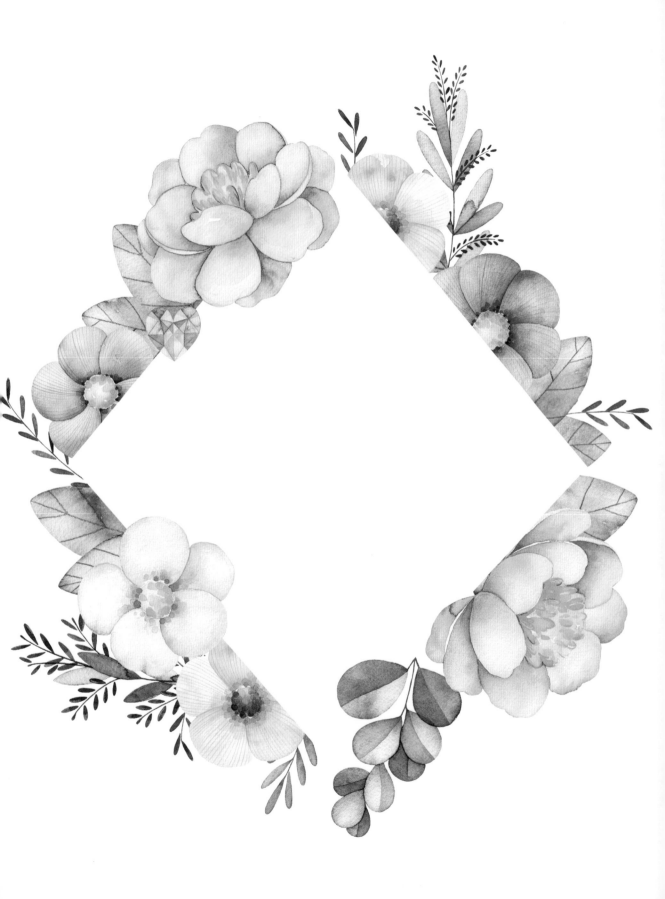

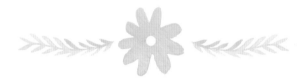

THICK 'N' THIN

The contrast of thick and thin lines made with a double-ended marker gives this alphabet a carefree feel. Thick 'n' Thin can be used for titles, captions or longer bodies of text in a range of letter sizes using the same colourful tools. These letters are written fairly carefully, but can be done quite quickly. They work well for recording childhood firsts or those memorable moments when kids are captivated by their toys or bond with new friends.

TOOLS

- Double-ended pigmented markers in various colours

Alternative tools:
- 0.50 mm pigmented fine-line marker and a medium-point permanent marker

LETTER-SPACING GUIDE

All letters sit on the baseline.

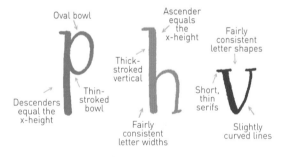

DISTINGUISHING FEATURES

The thin end of the marker is used for bowls and serifs, and the thick end for stronger verticals. Single-stroke letters such as i, l, o, s and t, and some numbers can be made either thick or thin to add interest and texture to your writing. This alphabet has ascenders and descenders equal in length to the x-height, and letters are vertical but not rigid. Letter shapes are fairly consistent in size and shape, with oval bowls and arches.

Oval bowl

Descenders equal the x-height

Thin-stroked bowl

Thick-stroked vertical

Fairly consistent letter widths

Ascender equals the x-height

Fairly consistent letter shapes

Short, thin serifs

Slightly curved lines

LETTER CONSTRUCTION

1. Use the thick end of a double-ended marker for the first vertical.

2. Use the thin end of the marker for the second stroke, making sure it overlaps the first one.

3. Still using the thin end of the marker, draw the third stroke so that it overlaps the second stroke and creates a counter space approximately equal to the first.

4. Use the thin end of the marker to add the serifs.

TIP

Use Thick 'n' Thin Capitals (pages 134–135) as the uppercase letters for this alphabet.

a b c d e f g

ascender

x-height

baseline

descender

h i j k l m n

o p q r s t u

v w x y z ? !

1 2 3 4 5 6 7 8 9 0

THICK 'N' THIN CAPITALS

These uppercase letters are designed to be used with the corresponding lowercase alphabet, but are also rather appealing when used alone. This letter style can be used for amusing captions or clever titles about trial and error or life's challenges. A range of letter sizes can be made using the same tools. The letters can be bounced up and down or tilted backward and forward a little for an even more cheerful look.

TOOLS

- Double-ended pigmented markers in various colours

Alternative tools:
- 0.50 mm pigmented fine-line marker and a medium-point permanent marker

LETTER-SPACING GUIDE

All letters sit on the baseline.

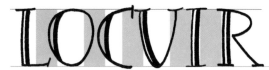

DISTINGUISHING FEATURES

Double-stroked verticals provide interesting contrast with the thin-line bowls. There are very few absolutely straight lines in this alphabet – even the verticals have a slight curve to them. The letters are fairly narrow and have compressed oval bowls. Slender serifs provide stability for thin-line strokes and also extend across the tops and bottoms of verticals to connect thick and thin strokes.

Top of bowls slope slightly downward

Thin serifs

Fairly consistent gap between the lines

All strokes have a slight curve

Fairly tall, narrow letters

Valley sits at about a quarter of the letter height

Contrasting thick and thin strokes

LETTER CONSTRUCTION

I. Use the thin end of a double-ended marker for the first three strokes. Note the slant of the first downward stroke.

2. Draw the second stroke so that the valley sits at about a quarter of the letter height.

3. Splay the third stroke a little more than the first to leave room for a contrasting thick stroke.

4. Use the thick end of the marker to make a stroke parallel to the left side of the second stroke.

5. Use the thick end of the marker to add a stroke parallel to the third one.

6. Use the thin end of the marker to add serifs connecting the contrasting strokes.

TIP

Use Thick 'n' Thin (pages 132–133) as the lowercase letters and numbers for this alphabet.

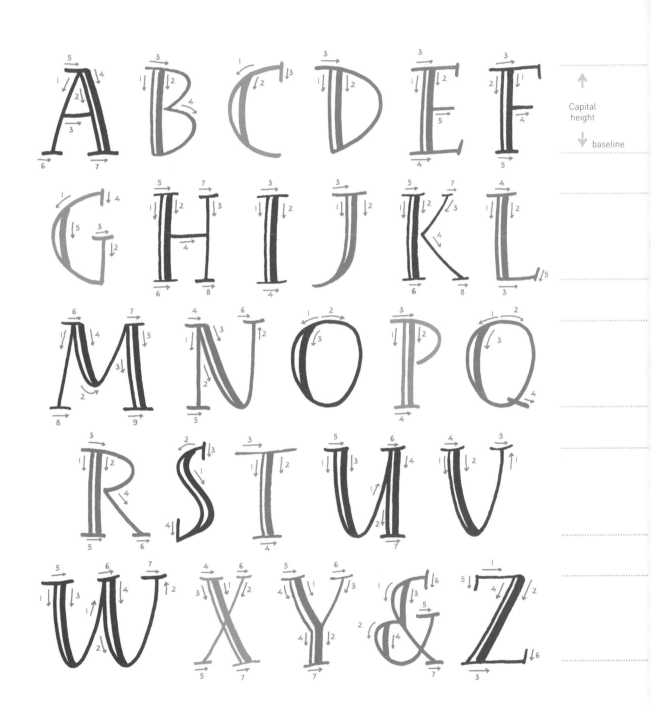

Capital
height

baseline

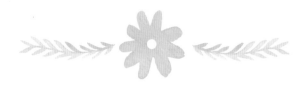

A B C D E F G H I J K L M N

↑
Capital
height

↓ baseline

a b c d e f g h i j k l m

↑
ascender

x-height
baseline
descender
↓

O P Q R S T U U V W X Y & Z

n o p q r s t u v w x y z

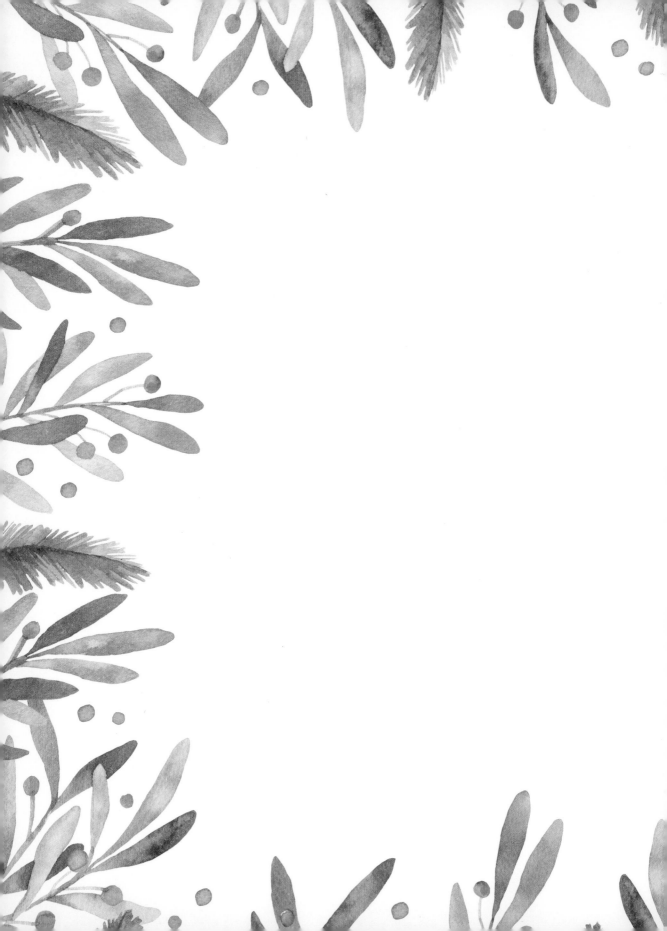

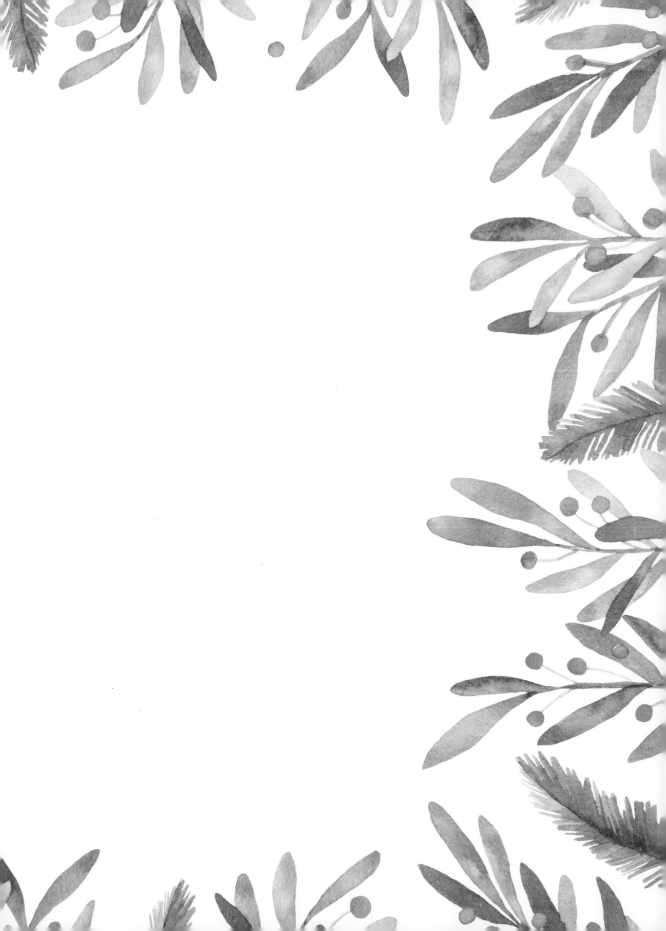

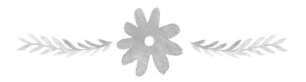

THORNTON

This confident and unique alphabet has a slightly quirky character that is ideal whenever bold statements or unusual captions are appropriate. A wonderful texture emerges when this letter style is used in a tightly woven text block. The alphabet is written with a broad-edged tool, so you should work slowly and always be aware of your pen angle. If you would like to create smaller or larger letters, change the size of the writing tool.

TOOLS

- 5.0 mm pigmented calligraphy marker

Alternative tools:
- Calligraphy fountain pen

LETTER-SPACING GUIDE

All letters sit on the baseline.

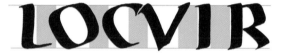

DISTINGUISHING FEATURES

This alphabet is built with rather unusual tilted square-shaped bowls. Letters are upright and stocky, written with an x-height equal to 4 nib widths. Short, pointed serifs are found at the tops and bottoms of the vertical strokes, and open letters have a manipulated 'tooth' serif. Thornton has no ascenders or descenders, so lines of text can be stacked quite closely together to create a bold and interesting texture.

Stocky letters
Unusual tilted square bowl
Straight, erect verticals
Bowl is wider at the bottom
Manipulated 'tooth' serif

Strong, overlapping joins
Short, pointed serifs
Upper counter space is larger than lower one

LETTER CONSTRUCTION

1. Using a 20° pen angle, make a short serif at the beginning of the vertical. Continue around the bottom curve, ending when the stroke becomes thin.

2. Begin the second stroke inside the first. Pull slightly right and down for about one-third of the x-height, then pull left for a thin exit stroke.

3. Start the third stroke so it overlaps the second. Pull slightly right and down the remaining two-thirds of the x-height, then pull left for a thin exit stroke that overlaps the thin end of the first stroke.

TIP

Thornton does not require a coordinating lowercase alphabet.

□ 20° dominant pen angle (all other pen angles are indicated next to the stroke)

4 nib widths

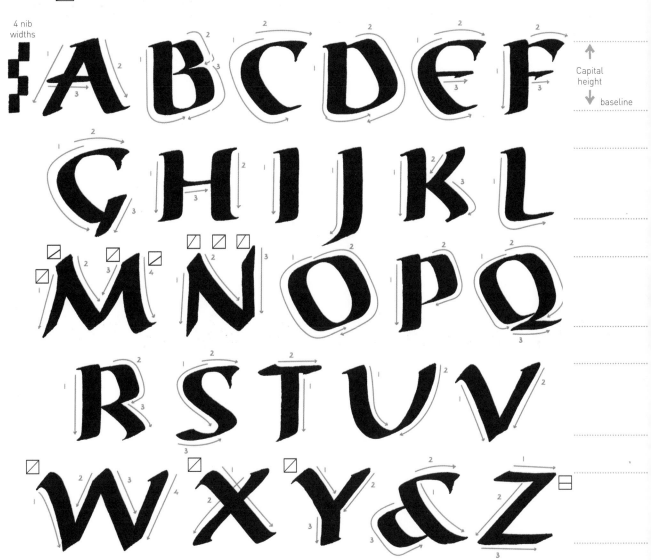

Capital height

baseline

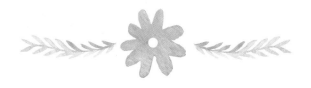

ABCDEFGHIJKLMN

↑
Capital
height
↓ baseline

OPQRSTUVWXY&Z

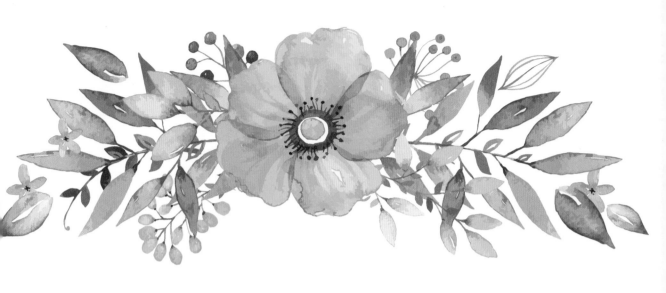

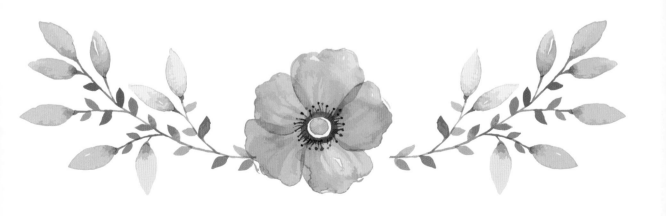

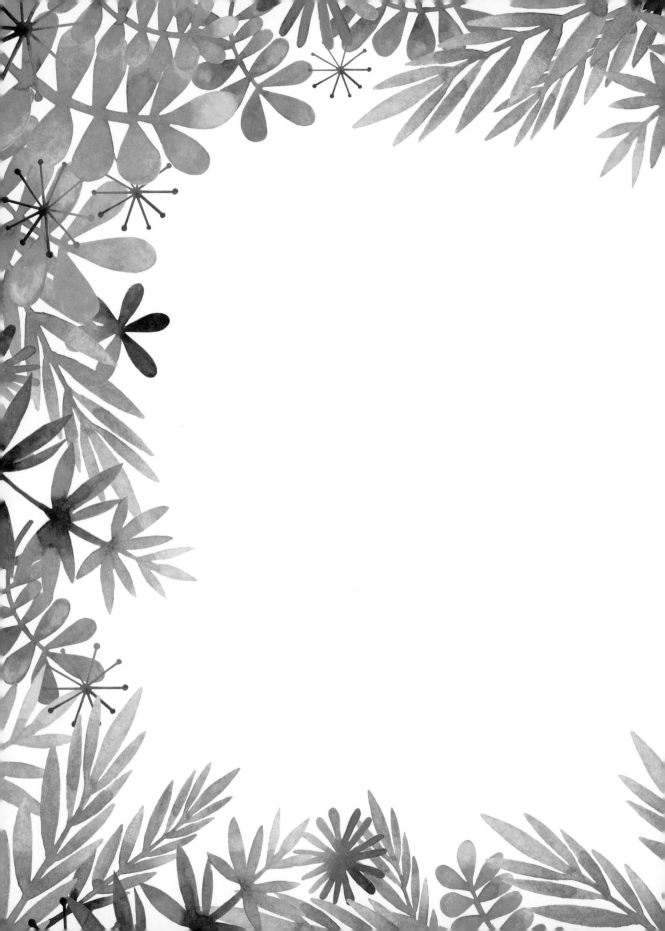

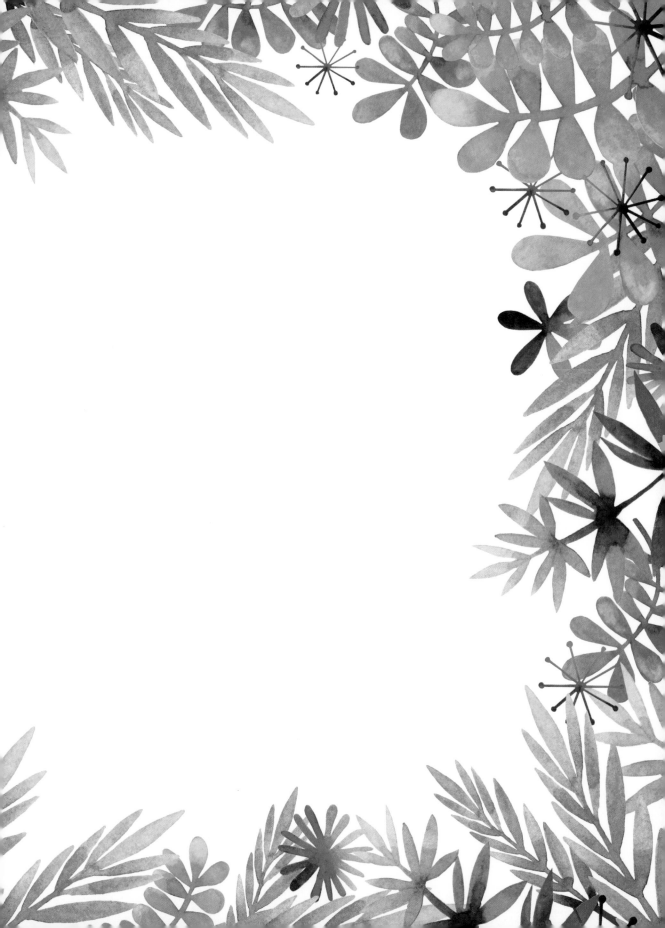

ITALIC

This popular calligraphic letter style has a sophisticated appeal but remains easy to read. You can use this alphabet for any special occasion, but it is especially appropriate for graduations, weddings and rites of passage. The letters are written with a broad-edged tool, so take special care that you work slowly and be aware of your pen angle. If you would like to create smaller or larger letters, you must change the size of your writing tool.

TOOLS

- 2.4 mm calligraphy fountain pen

Alternative tools:
- Broad-edged dip pen or calligraphy marker

LETTER-SPACING GUIDE

All letters sit on the baseline.

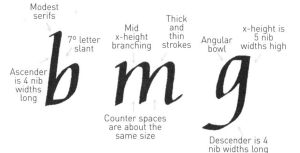

DISTINGUISHING FEATURES

These letters have an x-height of 5 nib widths, a dominant pen angle of about 35º and a forward letter slant of approximately 7º. The modest serifs and angular bowls are very consistent in size and shape, while the ascenders and descenders are slightly shorter than the x-height. The letter shapes are made with elegant thick and thin strokes that give this alphabet its 'black-tie' look.

Modest serifs
7º letter slant
Ascender is 4 nib widths long
Mid x-height branching
Thick and thin strokes
Counter spaces are about the same size
Angular bowl
x-height is 5 nib widths high
Descender is 4 nib widths long

LETTER CONSTRUCTION

35º 35º 35º

1. Pull a short, thin stroke to begin. Maintain a consistent pen angle throughout the curve to achieve contrasting thick and thin strokes.

2. Start the second stroke so that it overlaps the first for a strong join.

3. Pull the third stroke downward at a 7º slant, allowing it to overlap the first two strokes. Pull upward for a thin exit stroke.

TIP

Use Italic Capitals (pages 148–149) as the uppercase letters for this alphabet.

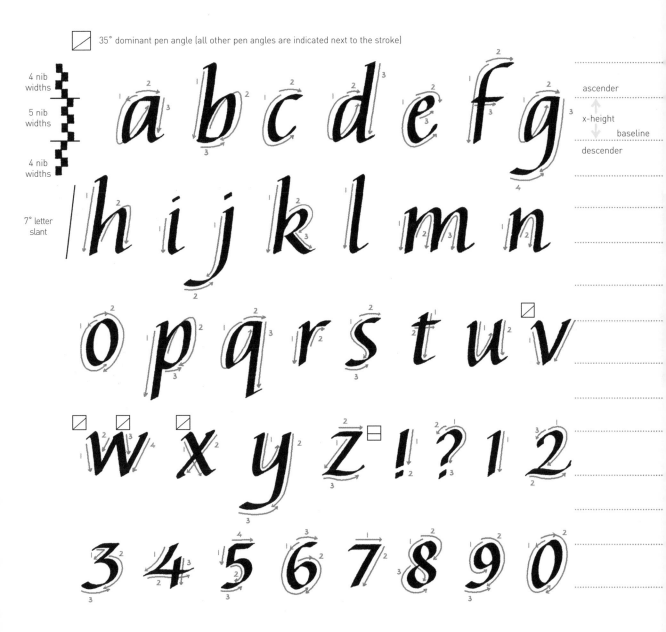

35° dominant pen angle (all other pen angles are indicated next to the stroke)

4 nib widths

5 nib widths

4 nib widths

7° letter slant

ascender

x-height

baseline

descender

ITALIC CAPITALS

This alphabet is designed to accompany the lowercase Italic letters, but can also be used on its own for titles or accent words. The calligraphic nature of this alphabet produces a refined look, making it appropriate for benchmark moments such as christenings, bar mitzvahs or college balls. Take special care that you work slowly and always be aware of your pen angle. Use a different-sized tool if you would like to create this alphabet at a different x-height.

TOOLS

- 2.4 mm calligraphy fountain pen

Alternative tools:
- Broad-edged dip pen or calligraphy marker

LETTER-SPACING GUIDE

All letters sit on the baseline.

LOCVIR

DISTINGUISHING FEATURES

These letters are written at a height of 7 nib widths, with a dominant pen angle of approximately 25º and a forward slant of about 7º. They have oval-shaped bowls and modest serifs. The broad-edged tool gives these letters their elegant thick and thin lines. Experienced calligraphers may wish to add a flourish to accent the first letter in a body of text. All letters sit on the baseline, but oval bowls and the points of diagonal strokes break the guidelines.

Pen manipulated to create 'tooth' serif — Oval counter space — Curve breaks the guidelines

Modest serifs — 7º letter slant — Upper bowl is smaller than lower bowl

Equal counter spaces — Points break the guidelines — Thick and thin strokes

LETTER CONSTRUCTION

1. Begin with a serif, then complete the vertical stroke. Pause at the baseline, then pull right and slightly up until the stroke thins.

2. Start the second stroke so that it overlaps the first at the top and stops just above centre height.

3. Start and end the third stroke so that it overlaps the thin ends of both the first and second strokes.

TIP

Use Italic (pages 146–147) as the lowercase letters and numbers for this alphabet.

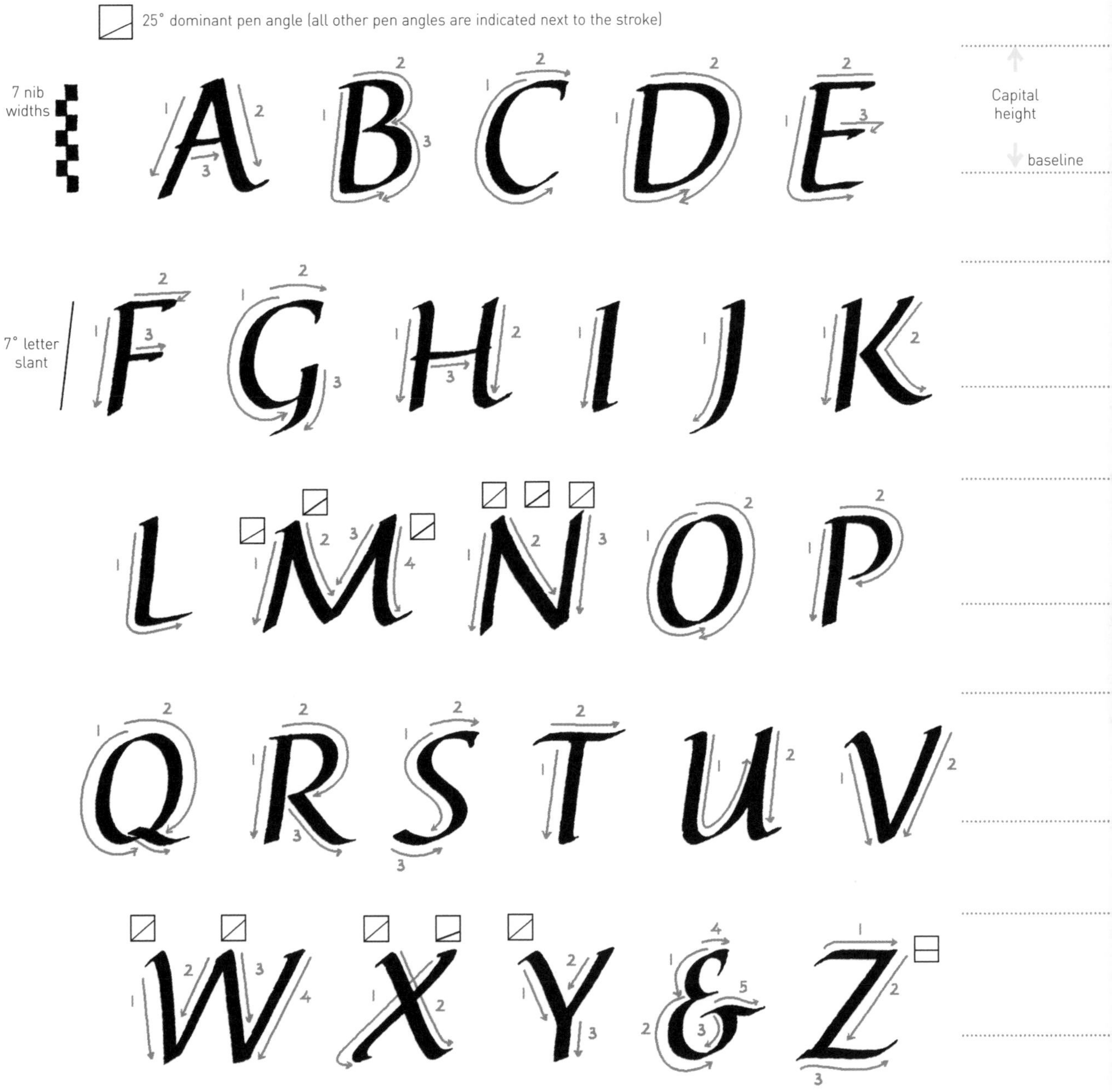

25° dominant pen angle (all other pen angles are indicated next to the stroke)

7 nib widths

Capital height

baseline

A B C D E

7° letter slant

F G H I J K

L M N O P

Q R S T U V

W X Y & Z

A B C D E F G H I J K L M N

↑

Capital
height

↓ baseline

a b c d e f g h i j k l m

↑
ascender

x-height
baseline
descender
↓

O P Q R S T U V W X Y &Z

n o p q r s t u v w x y z

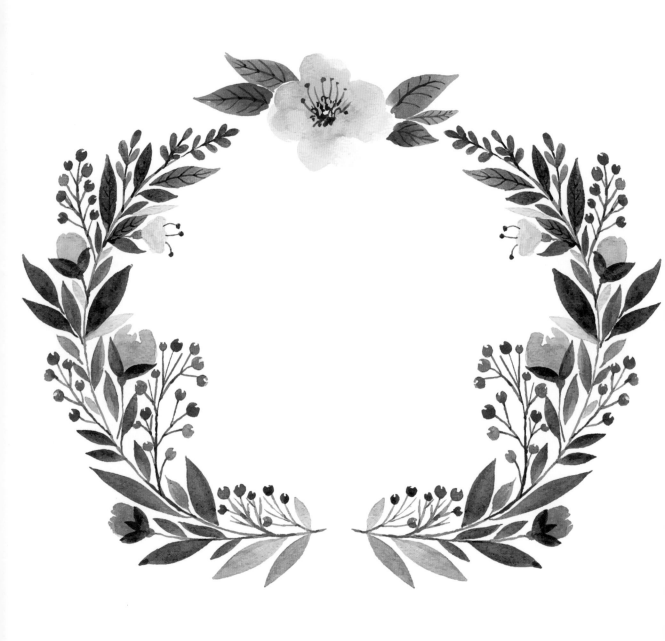

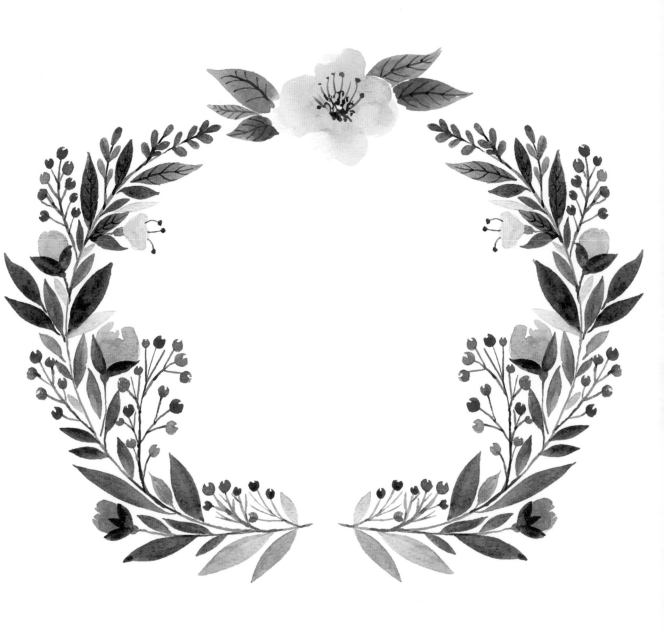

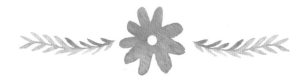

LYRIS

This is a kind-spirited alphabet with gentle nobility. Its character comes from a mixture of upper- and lowercase letter forms, most tall and thin but some wide, adding interesting texture to a body of text. It is appropriate for titles and captions, but also works for longer bodies of text, and is perfect for descriptions of ski trips, humorous captions or sweet poetry. Try fibre-tipped brushes in a variety of sizes for lettering at different heights.

● TOOLS

- Fibre-tipped brush marker with 10-mm (⅜-inch) long tapered tip
- Any monoline writing tool

● LETTER–SPACING GUIDE

All letters sit on the baseline.

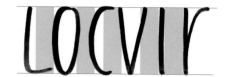

● DISTINGUISHING FEATURES

Tall, thin letters with a sprinkling of wide letters give this alphabet a lovely texture when used in larger blocks of text. The alphabet includes a mixture of sans-serif upper- and lowercase letters, including alternative forms of the letters e, n and t. Some letters have very high crossbars, while others have very low ones. The brush marker allows you to add extra interest by introducing some modest contrast of thick and thin strokes. The letters are relaxed a little by adding a slight curve to most vertical strokes.

Mix of upper- and lowercase letters

High crossbar

Moderate thick/thin contrast

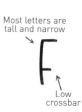

Most letters are tall and narrow

Low crossbar

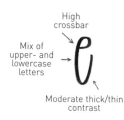

Verticals are slightly curved

A few letters are very wide

● LETTER CONSTRUCTION

1. Position the brush marker as shown. Apply pressure and then pull a slightly curved diagonal that extends about two-thirds of the letter height.

2. Position the brush marker as shown. Apply pressure and then pull a slightly curved second stroke, ending so that it overlaps the first stroke.

3. Position the brush marker and apply pressure before pulling a short vertical stroke.

a B C D E e

F O H I J K

L M N N O

P Q r S T t U

V W X Y e Z

↑ Capital height

↓ baseline

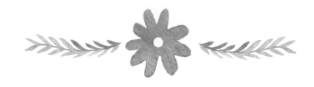

ABCDEFGHIJKLMN

↑

Capital
height

↓ baseline

NOPQRSTUVWXYZ

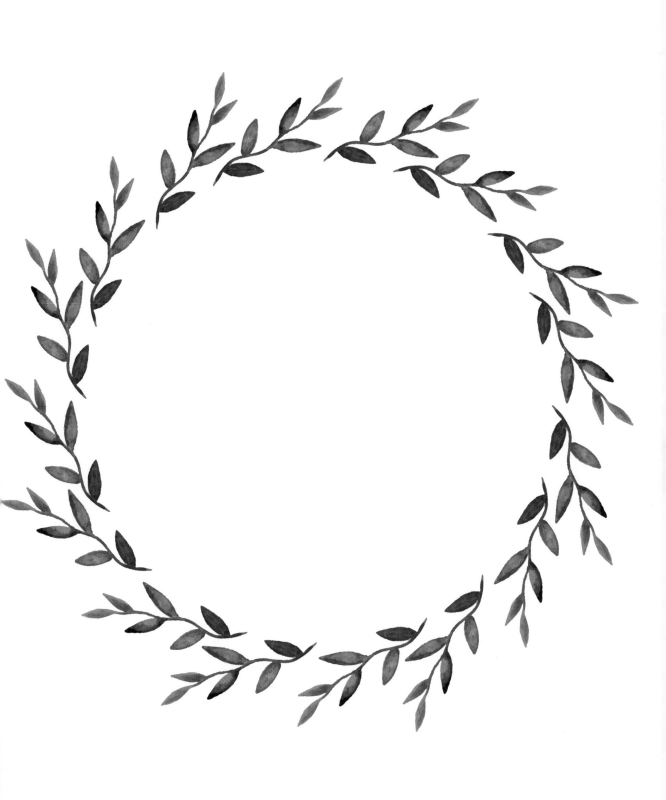

ROMAN MINUSCULES

Roman Minuscules is a variation of a standard calligraphic letter style. This round alphabet is practical, easy to read and gives a formal look to long bodies of text. It is also fitting for captions, labels or descriptions about formal occasions and noteworthy accomplishments. To achieve letters with the same proportions, you must use an appropriately sized calligraphic tool whenever this alphabet is penned at a different size.

TOOLS

- 3.0 mm pigmented calligraphy marker

Alternative tools:
- Traditional calligraphy dip pen or calligraphy fountain pen

LETTER-SPACING GUIDE

All letters sit on the baseline.

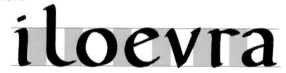

DISTINGUISHING FEATURES

Classic thick and thin strokes are achieved by using a broad-edged lettering tool. Letters are vertical, have round bowls and arches and modest hooked serifs. Ascenders and descenders are 2.5 nib widths and the x-height is 4.5 nib widths. Careful attention must be given to pen angles and letter construction to create this letter style.

Classic letter shapes

Vertical letters

Lower bowl is oval and slightly wider than upper bowl

x-height is 4.5 nib widths

Round bowl

Descender is 2.5 nib widths long

Ascender is 2.5 nib widths long

Round arch

Modest hook serifs

LETTER CONSTRUCTION

1. Using a pen angle of 30º, make a horizontal stroke from left to right.

2. Flatten the pen angle to about 0º for the diagonal stroke, allowing it to overlap the first stroke.

3. Steepen the pen angle back to 30º for the bottom horizontal, which should overlap the second stroke.

TIP

Use Roman Majuscules (pages 162–163) as the uppercase letters for this alphabet.

30° dominant pen angle (all other pen angles are indicated next to the stroke)

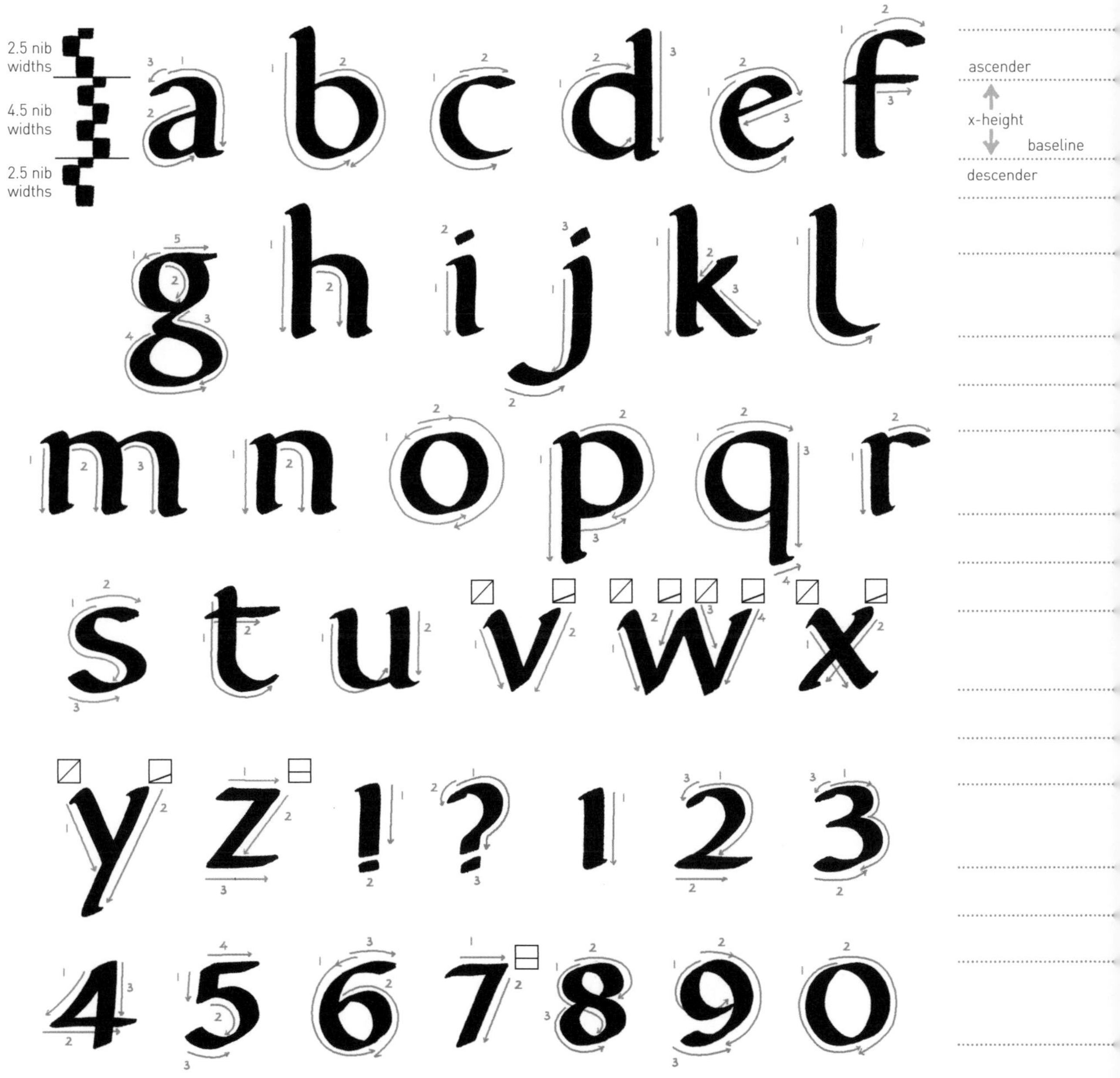
2.5 nib widths
4.5 nib widths
2.5 nib widths
ascender
x-height
baseline
descender

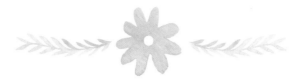

ROMAN MAJUSCULES

These carefully constructed letters have similar proportions to those found on the Trajan Column in Rome. They can be used alone for titles of monumental importance, or in combination with the lowercase Roman Minuscules for captions and text. This letter style is quite conservative and appropriate for honouring life achievements. A different size of tool is required if you would like to letter this alphabet at a different height.

TOOLS

- 3.0 mm pigmented calligraphy marker

Alternative tools:
- Traditional calligraphy dip pen or calligraphy fountain pen

LETTER-SPACING GUIDE

All letters sit on the baseline.

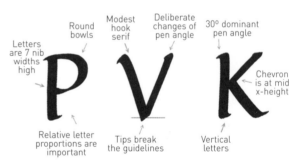

DISTINGUISHING FEATURES

These vertical letters with modest hooked serifs are written at a height of 7 nib widths and a dominant pen angle of 30º. Round bowls and the points of diagonal letters should break the guidelines, because otherwise these letters will look smaller than the others, even though in reality they would not be. Be conscious of pen angles and of how each stroke begins and ends. Relative letter widths are also intrinsic to the classic look of this alphabet.

Letters are 7 nib widths high

Round bowls

Modest hook serif

Deliberate changes of pen angle

30º dominant pen angle

Chevron is at mid x-height

Relative letter proportions are important

Tips break the guidelines

Vertical letters

LETTER CONSTRUCTION

1. Using a 45º pen angle, begin with a hook serif and then pull a diagonal stroke for about two-thirds of the letter height.

2. Changing to a pen angle of about 20º, begin with a small hooked serif and then pull the second diagonal stroke.

3. Use a pen angle of about 30º for the final vertical stroke. Finish this stroke with a hooked serif.

TIP

Use Roman Minuscules (pages 160–161) as the lowercase letters and numbers for this alphabet.

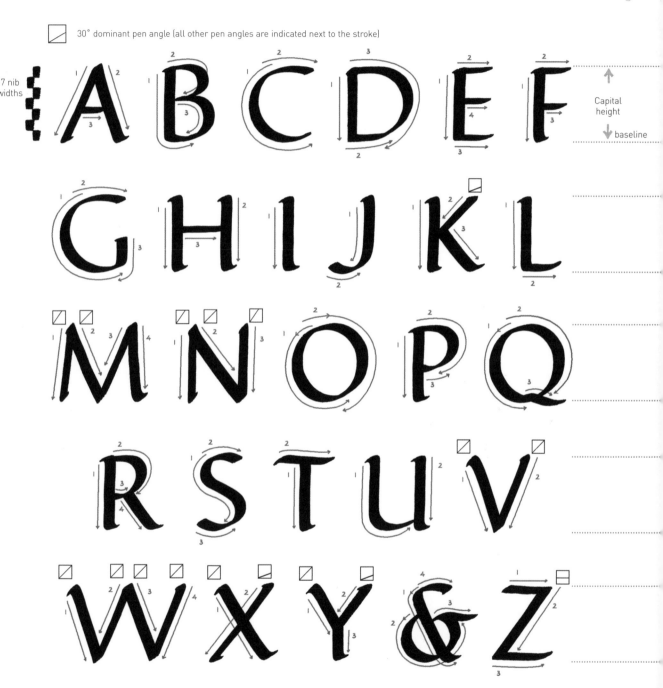

30° dominant pen angle (all other pen angles are indicated next to the stroke)

7 nib widths

Capital height

baseline

a b c d e f g h i j k l m

↑
ascender

x-height

baseline

descender
↓

A B C D E F G H I J K L M N

↑
Capital
height

↓ baseline

n o p q r s t u v w x y z

O P Q R S T U V W X Y & Z

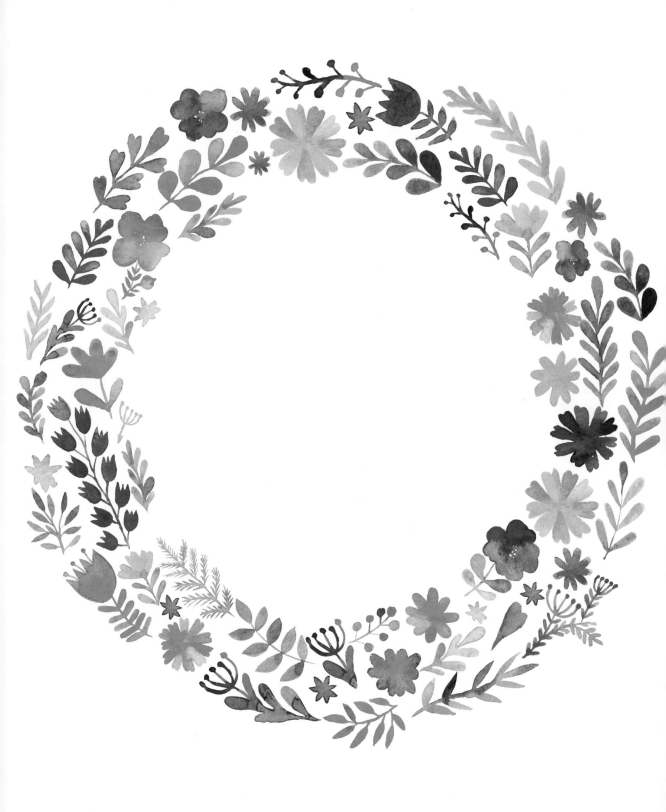

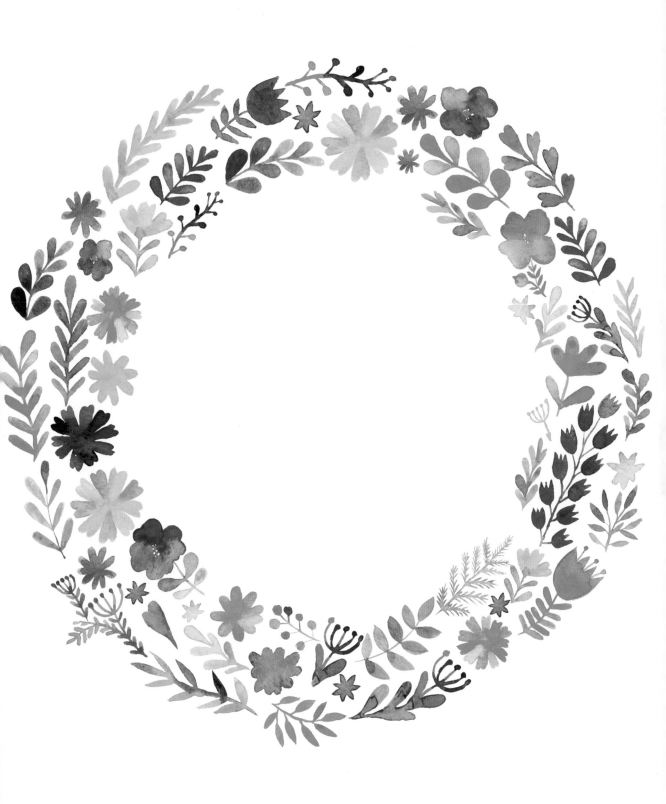

UTOPIA

This alphabet is perfect for title pages and short captions about everyday fun and life's warm moments. Utopia is a monocase alphabet, so there is no need to learn both upper- and lowercase letters. Although the use of a pointed brush pen makes this letter style more challenging, a range of letter sizes can be made with the same tool. Try to maintain a fairly consistent letter weight within a body of text when using this tool, because minor changes in pressure will result in heavier- or lighter-weight letters.

TOOLS

- Pointed brush pen

Alternative tools:
- Experiment with the brush to see what range of letter sizes it can make.

LETTER-SPACING GUIDE

All letters sit on the baseline.

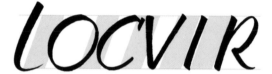

DISTINGUISHING FEATURES

Low-branching letters have rounded bowls that are slightly wider at the top than at the bottom. This shape allows the letters to be quite closely packed together, often touching one another at their widest points. Some letters have a short horizontal lead-in stroke or foot to give them more stability. The alphabet has short ascenders and descenders, allowing the use of less space between lines of text. A lovely mix of upper- and lowercase letter forms gives this style a warm and friendly feel.

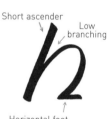

Short ascender
Low branching
Horizontal foot for stability

Rounded counter space is narrower at the bottom
Short descender

Serif created with brush tip
20° letter slant
Compressed Uncial-like shape

LETTER CONSTRUCTION

I. Position the brush as shown and apply pressure to produce a broad vertical stroke.

2. Turn the brush clockwise and apply less pressure for a narrower second stroke.

3. Apply more pressure to begin a broader third stroke. Release the pressure as you move around the curve, then increase it as you go up.

4. Turn the brush perpendicular to the baseline, apply some pressure and add a short, horizontal serif.

20° letter slant

Capital height

baseline

A B C D E F

G H I J K L

M N O P Q R

S T U V W X

Y Z ! ? 1 2 3

4 5 6 7 8 9 0

A B C D E F G H I J K L M

Capital
height
baseline

N O P Q R S T U V W X Y Z

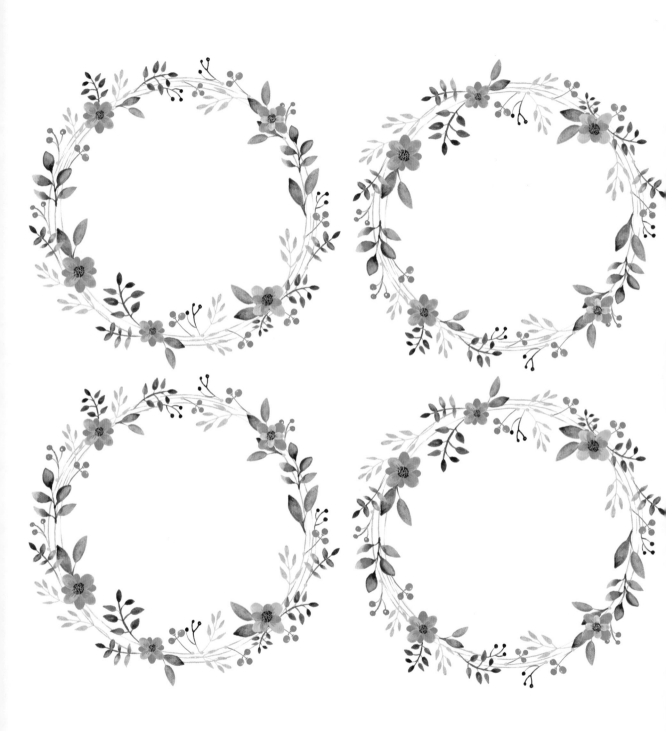

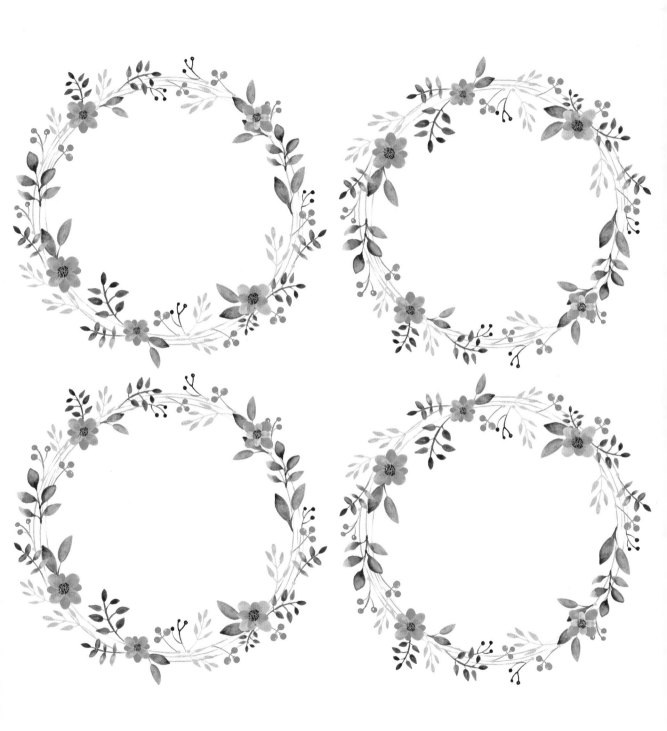

SCHOOLBOOK

This familiar and legible alphabet is written with easy-to-handle tools. This style can be used for long text, simple captions or lengthy quotes and is just as appropriate for recording school memories as it is for sports events. To create larger letters, use a larger marker.

TOOLS

- 0.5 mm pigmented fine-line marker

Alternative tools:
- Coloured fine-line markers, coloured pencils or gel pens

LETTER-SPACING GUIDE

All letters sit on the baseline.

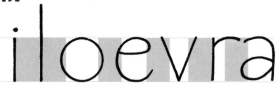

DISTINGUISHING FEATURES

Schoolbook is a monoline alphabet based on traditional Roman minuscules. It is written slowly and methodically, but the tools and letter shapes are familiar. Vertical letters have strong arches and round bowls that are very consistent in size and shape. The ascenders and descenders for this letter style are the same length as the x-height.

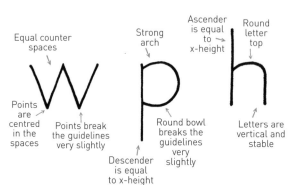

Equal counter spaces

Points are centred in the spaces

Points break the guidelines very slightly

Strong arch

Round bowl breaks the guidelines very slightly

Descender is equal to x-height

Ascender is equal to x-height

Round letter top

Letters are vertical and stable

LETTER CONSTRUCTION

1. Draw the first stroke of the small, round upper bowl, which should be about three-quarters of the x-height.

2. Complete the bowl so that the second stroke overlaps the first.

3. Start the third stroke so that it overlaps the others, creating a horizontal oval lower bowl that is wider than the upper bowl.

4. Pull the last stroke almost flat and along the top guideline. Keep it short.

TIP

Use Schoolbook Capitals (pages 176–177) as the uppercase letters for this alphabet.

a b c d e f g

ascender

x-height

baseline

descender

h i j k l m n

o p q r s t u

v w x y z ? !

1 2 3 4 5 6 7 8 9 0

SCHOOLBOOK CAPITALS

Schoolbook Capitals is a standard alphabet with classic proportions. This style can be used alone for neat titles, captions and banners, or as the uppercase letters to accompany the lowercase Schoolbook. This alphabet works well on scrapbook pages that require a lot of short phrases or labels. To create larger letters, use a larger marker.

● TOOLS

- 0.50 mm pigmented fine-line marker

Alternative tools:
- Coloured fine-line markers, coloured pencils or gel pens

● LETTER–SPACING GUIDE

All letters sit on the baseline.

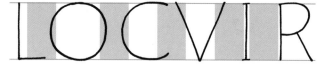

● DISTINGUISHING FEATURES

Schoolbook Capitals should be written slowly and carefully, but the tools are familiar and the letter shapes widely recognized. It is based on traditional Roman majuscules, with upright letters and very consistent round bowls. Take special care that you maintain the relative proportions of this alphabet's letters. These are not block letters; some letters are quite wide, while others are relatively narrow.

Bowl extends from the top of the vertical

Upper bowl is slightly smaller than lower bowl

Points pierce the guidelines

Open at top and bottom rather than curled in

Both bowls begin and end at the vertical

Vertical letters with no slant

Full, round counter space

● LETTER CONSTRUCTION

1. Draw the first stroke with a very slight curve to the left.

2. Start the second stroke so that it overlaps the first, again curving it very slightly.

3. Start the third stroke so that it overlaps the second. This is also slightly curved.

4. Draw the final stroke with a slight curve outward.

TIP

Use Schoolbook (pages 174–175) as the lowercase letters and numbers for this alphabet.

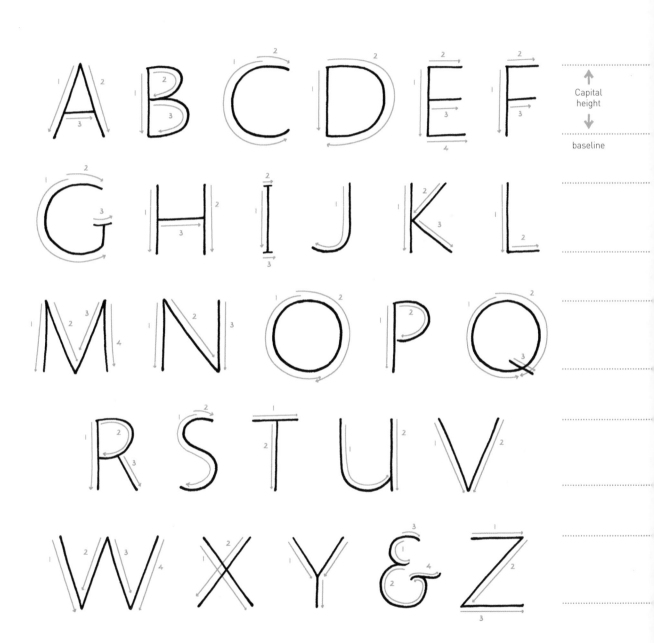

Capital height

baseline

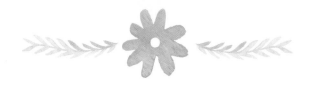

A B C D E F G H I J K L M N

↑
Capital
height

↓ baseline

a b c d e f g h i j k l m

↑
ascender

x-height
baseline
descender
↓

O P Q R S T U V W X Y & Z

n o p q r s t u v w x y z

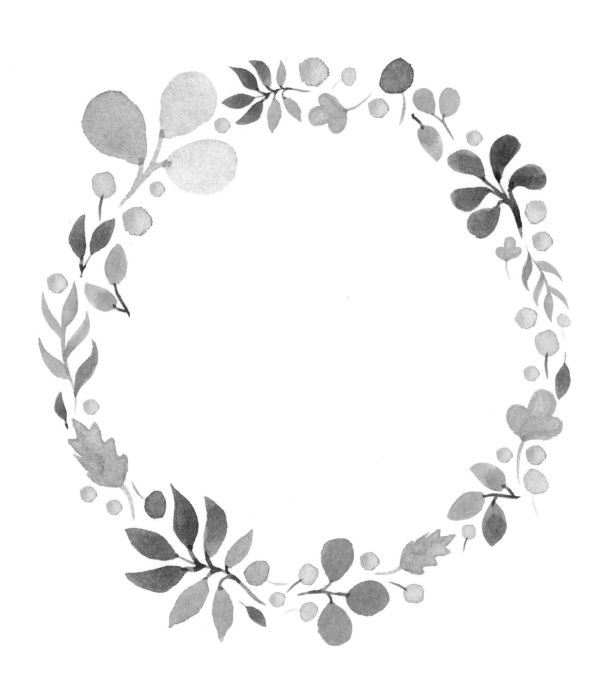

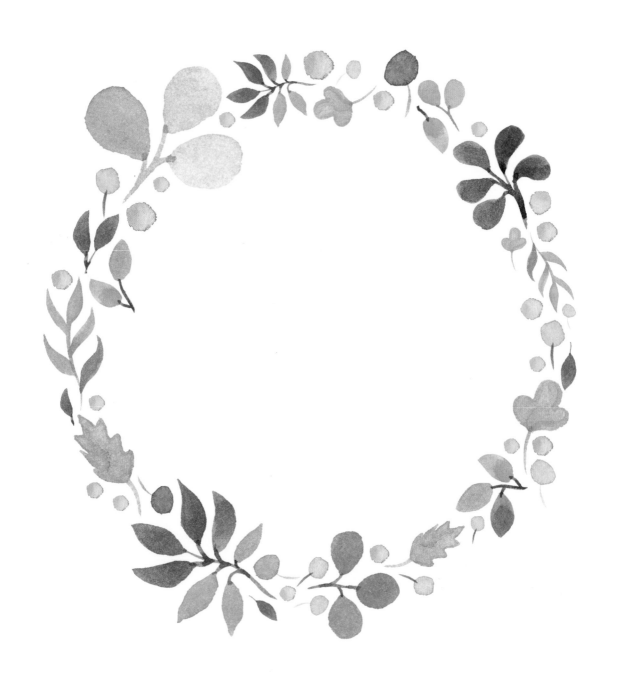

DIANNAH

This calligraphic hybrid features the graceful branching of Italic (pages 146–147) and the round, open feel of Uncial (pages 190–191), giving character and warmth to this otherwise formal-looking letter style. This alphabet is appropriate for grand stories of loyal friendships and family histories, and can be used for titles, captions and longer bodies of text. A different-sized calligraphic tip is required if you would like to write smaller or larger.

● TOOLS

- 2.4 mm calligraphy fountain pen

Alternative tools:
- Traditional broad-edged dip pen or calligraphy marker

● LETTER-SPACING GUIDE

Letters sit on the baseline and serifs break through it.

iloevra

● DISTINGUISHING FEATURES

This is a calligraphic alphabet with a dominant pen angle of 25º, an x-height of 5 nib widths and a slight forward slant of about 3º. Ascenders have modest hook serifs, while descenders have simple hairline serifs. Rounded bowls and mid x-height branching are combined to create teardrop-shaped bowls, while a traditional round o and c help relate this alphabet to the uppercase Roman Majuscules (pages 162–163).

Ascender has a hook serif ↘

Ascender is shorter than x-height ↓

Thick and thin contrast

x-height equals 5 nib widths

Descender is shorter than x-height ↘

b

Teardrop-shaped counter space

n

Branching at mid x-height

Hairline serif

q

3º letter slant

● LETTER CONSTRUCTION

25º

25º

25º

1. Using a 25º pen angle throughout, make a hairline serif and then continue the stroke around and up almost to the top of the x-height.

2. Start the second stroke so that it overlaps the first stroke for about the first three-quarters of the x-height.

3. Add a hairline serif at the bottom of the second stroke.

TIP

Adapt Roman Majuscules (pages 162–163) to use as uppercase letters for Diannah.

◪ 25° dominant pen angle (all other pen angles are indicated next to the stroke)

3 nib widths

5 nib widths

3 nib widths

3° letter slant

ascender

x-height

baseline

descender

a b c d e f

g h i j k l

m n o p q r

s t u v w x

y z ! ? 1 2 3

4 5 6 7 8 9 0

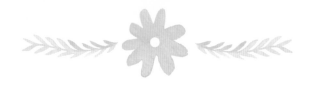

a b c d e f g h i j k l m

ascender

↑
x-height
↓   baseline

descender

n o p q r s t u v w x y z

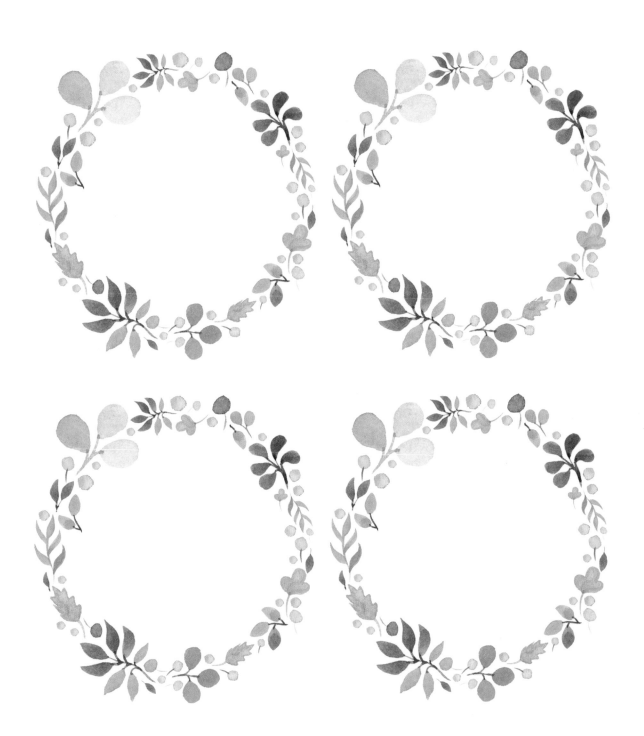

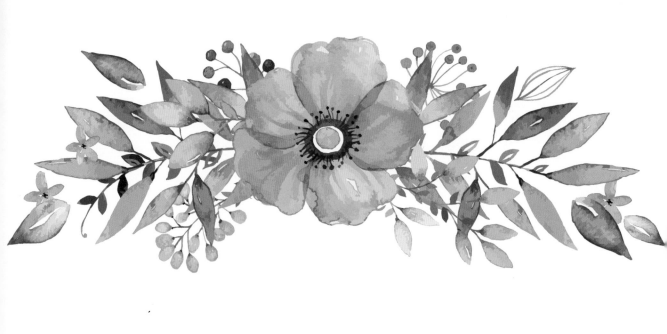

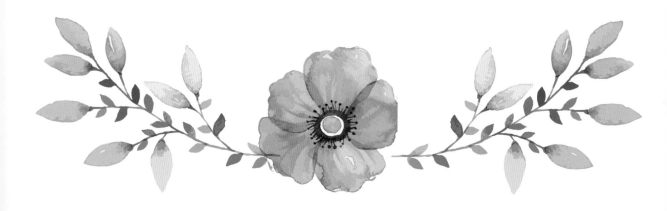

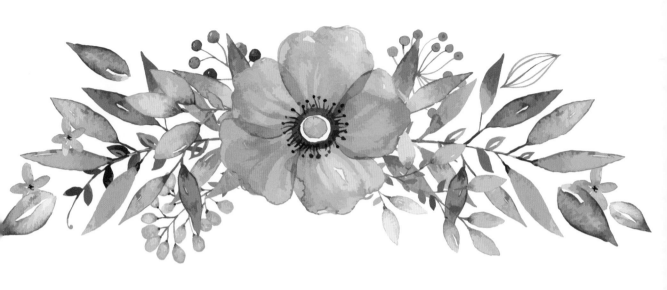

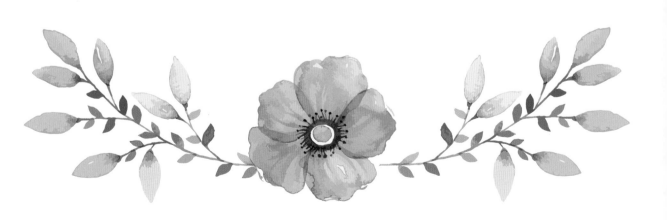

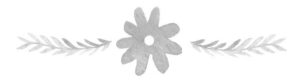

UNCIAL

This sturdy calligraphic alphabet is full of warmth and character. It can be used for a wide range of events, but seems just right to follow a boy or girl from childhood adventures to youthful accomplishments. It is appropriate for titles and captions, but also creates a lovely texture when used in a text block. Try to work slowly and be aware of your pen angle. If you would like to create smaller or larger letters, change the size of the writing tool.

TOOLS

- 3.5 mm pigmented calligraphy marker

Alternative tools:
- Calligraphy fountain pen or broad-edged dip pen

LETTER-SPACING GUIDE

All letters sit on the baseline.

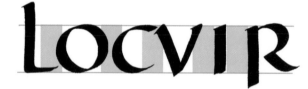

DISTINGUISHING FEATURES

This alphabet has strong, arching letters with large, round bowls and very simple, modest serifs. An interesting mix of upper- and lowercase letters as well as a few uncommon forms give Uncial a warm, friendly feel, while its calligraphic nature imbues it with a slightly more formal appeal. The alphabet has short ascenders and descenders, so less space is needed between lines of text.

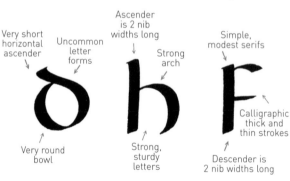

Very short horizontal ascender

Uncommon letter forms

Ascender is 2 nib widths long

Strong arch

Simple, modest serifs

Calligraphic thick and thin strokes

Very round bowl

Strong, sturdy letters

Descender is 2 nib widths long

LETTER CONSTRUCTION

1. Using a 20° pen angle, pull a short horizontal serif. Pause before continuing around the counter space.

2. Pull the second stroke to the left at the bottom so that it overlaps the first stroke to ensure a strong join.

3. Start the third stroke so that it overlaps the second stroke.

4. Complete the fourth stroke so that the thin end overlaps the thin end of the third stroke to make a strong join.

TIP

This is a monocase alphabet without separate upper- and lowercase letters.

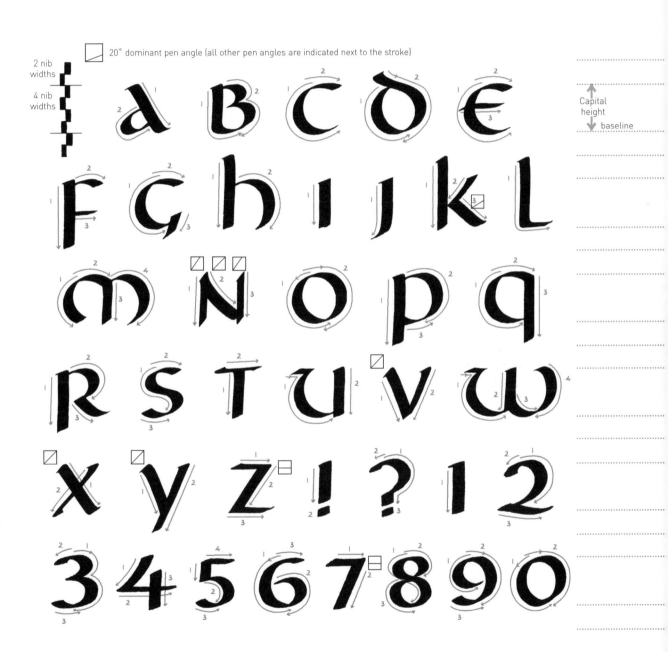

◰ 20° dominant pen angle (all other pen angles are indicated next to the stroke)

2 nib widths

4 nib widths

Capital height

baseline

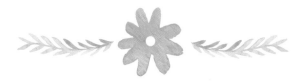

a b c d e f g h i j k l m n

Capital
height
baseline

o p q r s t u v w x y z

RUDY

Use this typeface for titling, short phrases or tightly packed blocks of text designed to leave an impression. Some practice may be required to master these letters because they are written using a calligraphic tool. Additionally, four of the letters require some pen manipulation. If you want to letter larger or smaller, use a different-sized calligraphic tool.

TOOLS

- 5.0 mm pigmented calligraphy marker

Alternative tools:
- Traditional calligraphy dip pen or calligraphy fountain pen

LETTER-SPACING GUIDE

All letters sit on the baseline.

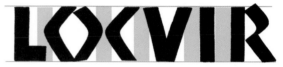

DISTINGUISHING FEATURES

These stocky sans-serif letters are written with an x-height of 4 nib widths. All verticals are made with a flat 0° pen angle and all horizontals with a 90° pen angle. The rounded bowls on B, D, O and Q require some pen manipulation; this means turning the handle of the pen clockwise while executing the stroke. The steadfast nature of this alphabet requires that the letters be very consistent in size and shape, and that all strokes land squarely on the baseline. Lines of text can be packed closely together to create a bold texture.

Flat (0°) dominant pen angle — Entire width of the strokes overlap

Letters are vertical — Horizontal strokes use a 90° pen angle

Unusual letter shapes — Pen angle is manipulated from 35° to about 0° — Strokes sit squarely on baseline

LETTER CONSTRUCTION

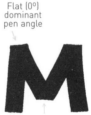

1. Beginning at the top, pull downward to create a vertical stroke using a flat (0°) pen angle.

2. Begin the second stroke with the left corner overlapping the first stroke and the right corner sitting above it. Curve the stroke to make a bowl that is about one-third of the letter height.

3. For the bottom bowl, start with a 35° pen angle, then rotate the pen clockwise between your thumb and forefinger so that the stroke ends on a flat pen angle.

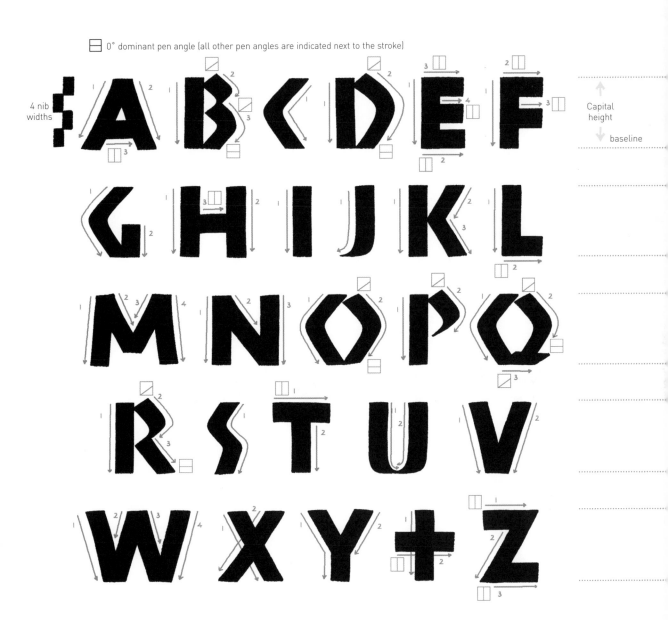

⊟ 0° dominant pen angle (all other pen angles are indicated next to the stroke)

4 nib widths

Capital height

baseline

ABCDEFGHIJKLMN

Capital
height

baseline

OPQRSTUVWXYZ

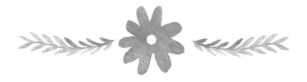

MORSE CODE

Dots and dashes suggest a text full of intrigue and coded messages. This style can be adapted to incorporate an endless variety of motifs to suit your memory pages. Created with familiar tools, these letters are easy but time-consuming to draw. Carefully sketch words lightly in pencil to provide a guide before adding the dots and dashes. This alphabet can easily be adapted for larger titles by using slightly larger pens.

● TOOLS

- 2H pencil
- 0.50 mm pigmented fine-line marker
- Soft white eraser

Alternative tools:
- Coloured pencils, coloured fine-line markers or gel pens

● LETTER-SPACING GUIDE

All letters sit on the baseline.

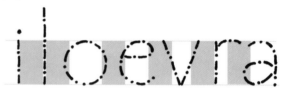

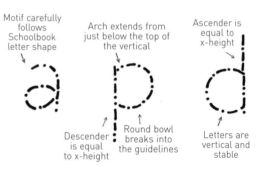

Motif carefully follows Schoolbook letter shape

Arch extends from just below the top of the vertical

Ascender is equal to x-height

Descender is equal to x-height

Round bowl breaks into the guidelines

Letters are vertical and stable

● DISTINGUISHING FEATURES

Morse Code is based on the Schoolbook alphabet to ensure legibility, so refer to pages 174–179 for guidance on drawing the underlying letter shapes. The dots and dashes are added quickly but carefully, giving the alphabet an interesting texture. Vertical letters with round bowls have ascenders and descenders that are equal in length to the letter's x-height. This alphabet can be adapted for an endless variety of themes by substituting other small, simple motifs for the dots and dashes.

● LETTER CONSTRUCTION

1. Using a pencil, lightly draw the underlying Schoolbook letter.

2. Using a fine-line marker, carefully add dashes and dots on top of the pencilled letter.

3. Wait for the ink to dry, then erase any noticeable pencil lines.

TIP

Use Schoolbook Capitals (pages 176–177) in conjunction with the instructions to create an uppercase Morse Code alphabet.

a b c d e f g

ascender

x-height

baseline

descender

h i j k l m n

o p q r s t u

v w x y z ? !

1 2 3 4 5 6 7 8 9 0

a b c d e f g h i j k l m

ascender

↑
x-height
↓ baseline

descender

n o p q r s t u v w x y z

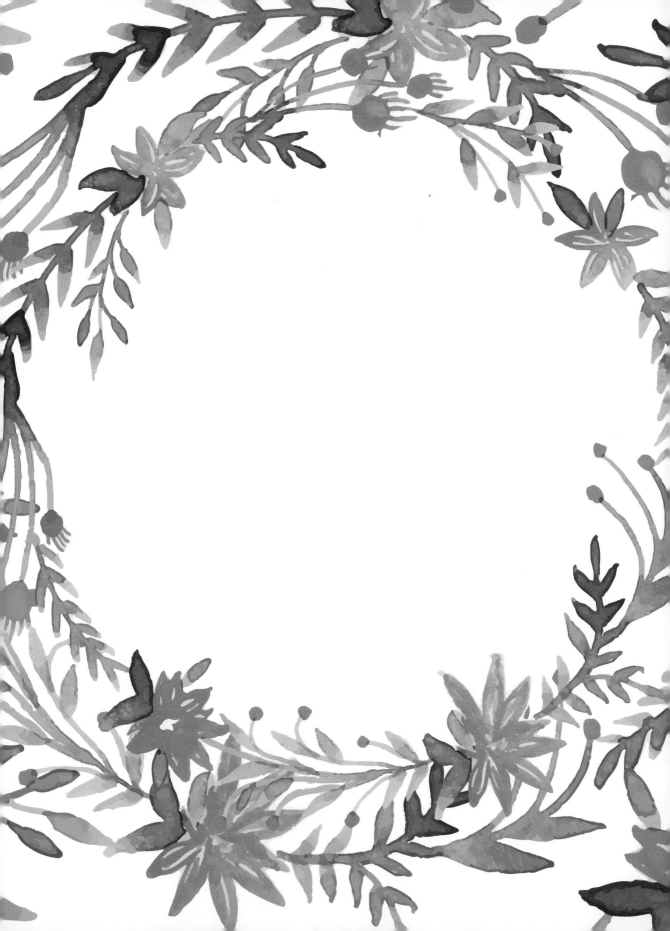

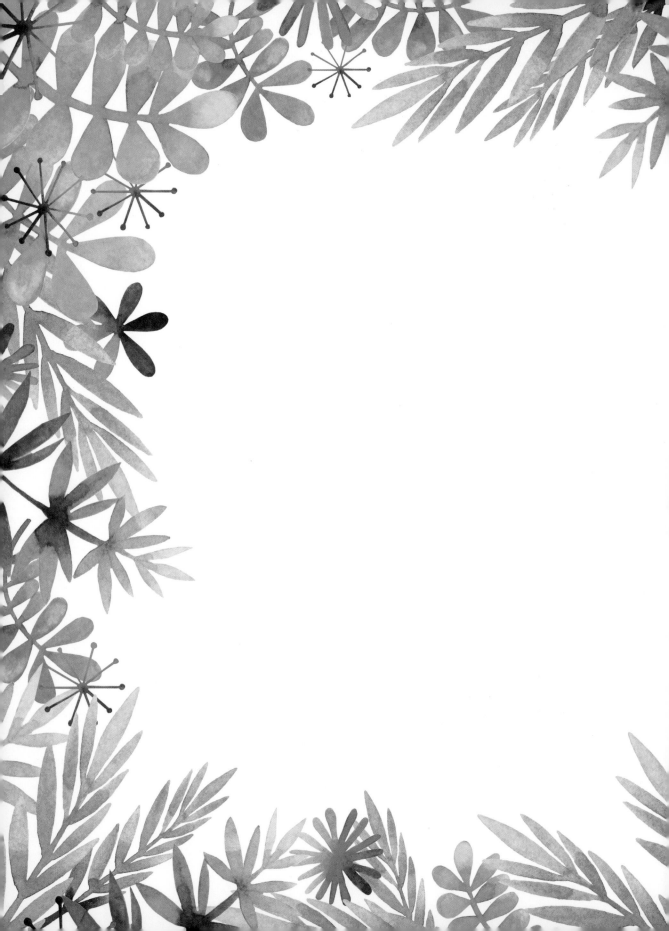

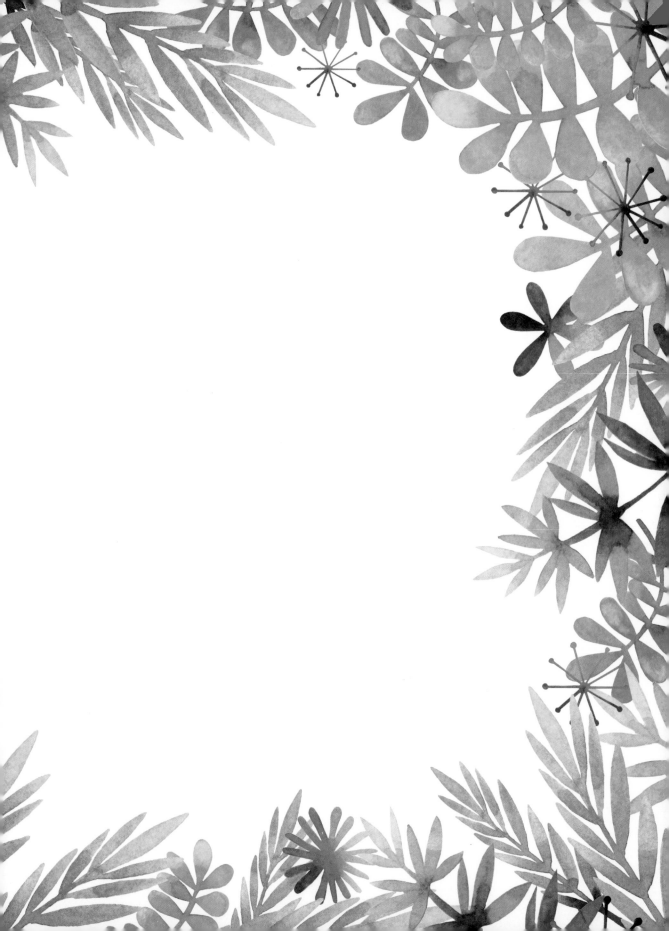

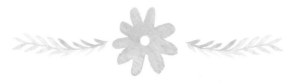

APPLIQUÉ

These cheerful letters will brighten up your scrapbook pages. The letters are drawn, outlined and filled in with a decorative element to give them a layered look. A variety of motifs are demonstrated here, but you can use any colour or pattern that suits your mood, as well as vary the size using the same tools. Lettering will look more homogenous if only one motif and a limited colour palette are used within a single body of text.

TOOLS

- H pencil
- 0.42 mm pigmented fine-line marker
- 0.10 mm pigmented fine-line marker
- Soft white eraser
- Coloured pencils

Alternative tools:
- Gel pens

DISTINGUISHING FEATURES

The letters are sketched lightly with pencil before being drawn with a fine-line marker and then outlined with a finer marker. The extra-fine outline gives the letters a layered look and adds a sweet handmade touch to this alphabet. The letters are upright and fairly consistent in shape, with round bowls and small counter spaces. Ascenders and descenders are about half the length of the x-height.

LETTER-SPACING GUIDE

All letters sit on the baseline.

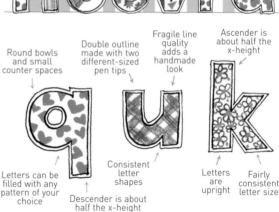

Round bowls and small counter spaces

Double outline made with two different-sized pen tips

Fragile line quality adds a handmade look

Ascender is about half the x-height

Letters can be filled with any pattern of your choice

Descender is about half the x-height

Consistent letter shapes

Letters are upright

Fairly consistent letter size

LETTER CONSTRUCTION

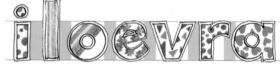

1. Use an H pencil to sketch the letter outline.

2. Ink in the letter shape with a fine-line marker, rotating the page whenever it is helpful.

3. Outline the letter with a finer marker. When the ink is dry, erase any noticeable pencil lines.

4. Fill in the letter with a motif of your choice. Notice that the finished letter is larger than the original pencil outline.

TIP

Adapt the letter shapes of
Schoolbook Capitals (pages
176–177) to use as uppercase
letters for Appliqué.

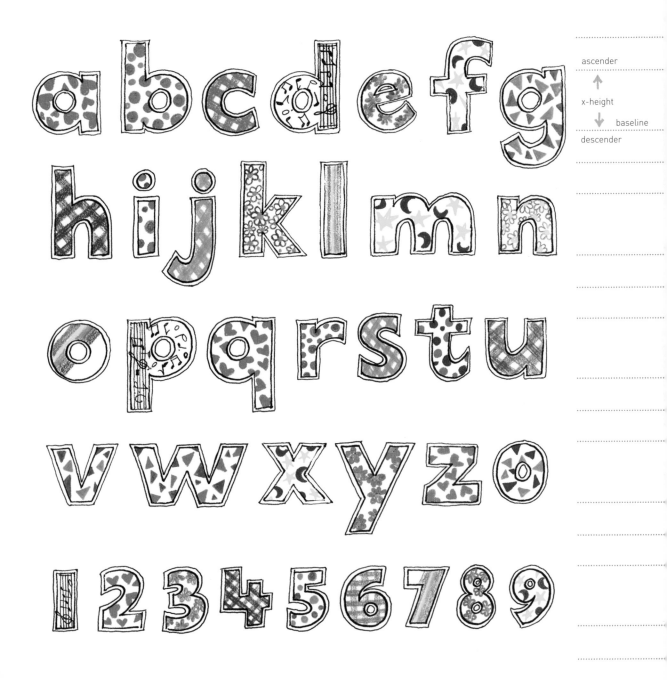

ascender

x-height

baseline

descender

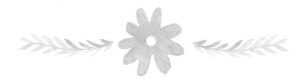

abcdefghijklmn

ascender

↑

x-height

↓ baseline

descender

opqrstuvwxyz

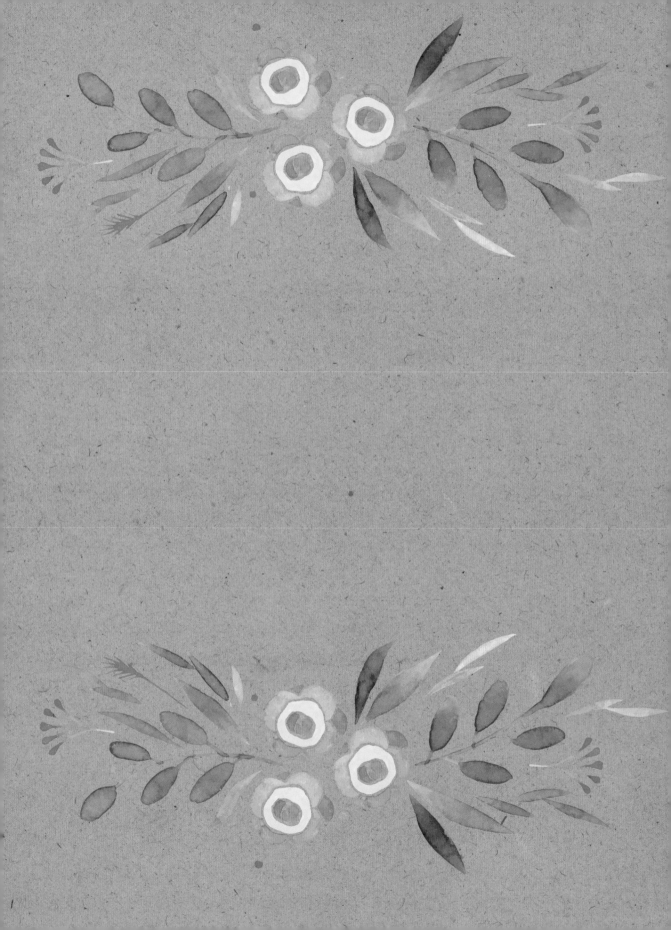

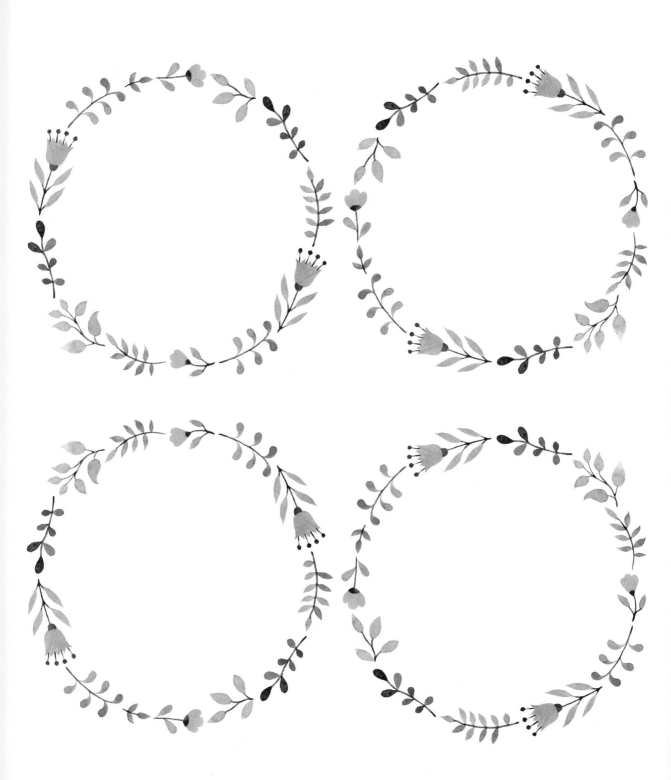

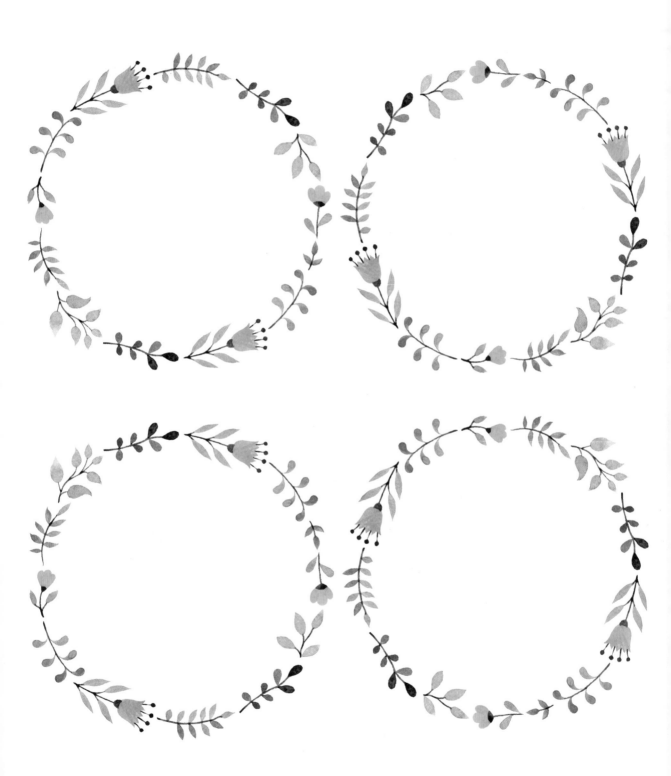

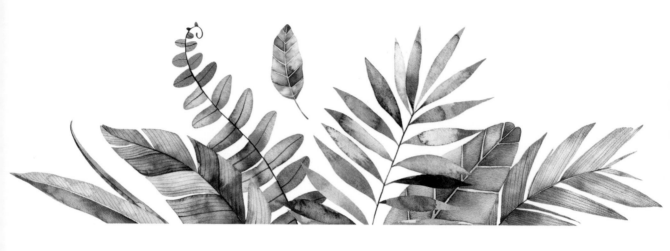
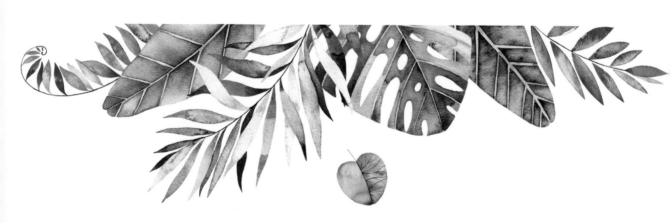

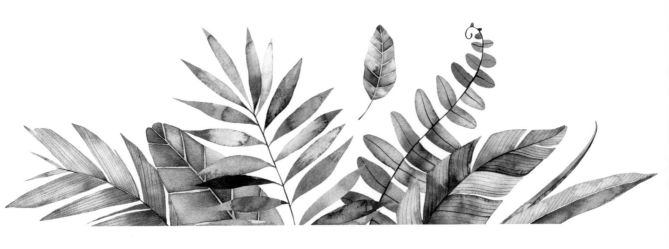

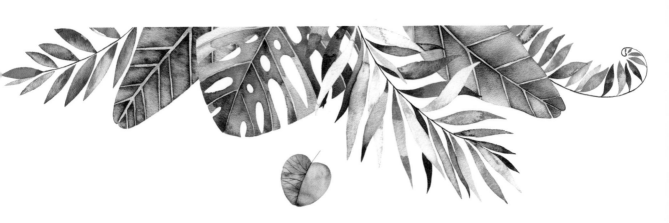

APPLIQUÉ

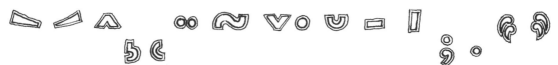

ART DECO, ART NOUVEAU, GRANDMA'S HANDWRITING, GRANDMA'S HANDWRITING CAPITALS, ISABELLA, MISS BARRETT, SCHOOLBOOK, MORSE CODE

ART DECO CAPITALS, ART NOUVEAU CAPITALS, ISABELLA CAPITALS, ONCE UPON A TIME, SCHOOLBOOK CAPITALS, STICK LETTER CAPITALS

BALLERINA, ITALIC, ITALIC CAPITALS

BRUSH EXPRESS, BRUSH EXPRESS CAPITALS, EASTERN BAZAAR

CURLS

DIANNAH, ROMAN MAJUSCULES, ROMAN MINUSCULES, UNCIAL

LYRIS

MADELINE, MADELINE CAPITALS, TROY

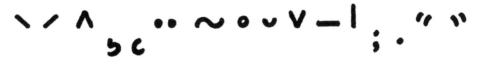

ROMEO

RUDY, THORNTON

SHOP FRONT

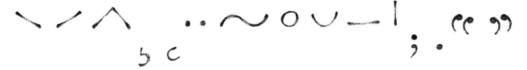

THICK 'N' THIN

THICK 'N' THIN CAPITALS

UTOPIA

TIP

Practise your accents and punctuation here.

GLOSSARY

ACIDIC Chemical term that indicates a pH value lower than 7.

ALKALINE A pH value higher than 7; also known as basic.

ARCH In a lowercase letter, the curved portion that attaches to the downstroke.

ASCENDER In a lowercase letter, the portion of the downstroke that extends above the x-height.

BASELINE Writing line or guideline on which the letters sit.

BLOCK LETTERS An alphabet with letters that are all about the same width.

BOWL The strokes that form the enclosed area of a letter.

BRANCHING STROKE In a lowercase letter, the section that springs up and out from within the downstroke.

BROAD-EDGED TOOL A tool having a writing tip with some width; calligraphy pen.

CALLIGRAPHIC Refers to letter styles made with a broad-edged writing tool.

CAPITAL HEIGHT The height of an uppercase letter.

COUNTER SPACE The partially or fully enclosed portion of a letter.

DESCENDER In a lowercase letter, the portion of the downstroke that extends below the x-height.

DOMINANT PEN ANGLE The pen angle used most often for a particular alphabet (see also Pen angle).

DOUBLE STROKE Two parallel strokes made with different-sized tools.

DOWNSTROKE A stroke made when the tool is moved from top to bottom.

DUCTUS The direction and order of the strokes that form a letter.

ENTRY STROKE The first mark your pen makes when beginning a letter.

EXIT STROKE The last mark your pen makes when finishing a letter.

FLICK A quick wrist motion; often used in brush lettering.

FLOURISH A decorative addition to a letter that extends beyond the letter shape.

GUIDELINES Temporary lines ruled to assist in making consistently sized letters in a straight line.

HAIRLINE SERIF The thinnest entry or exit stroke a pen can make.

HOOK SERIF An entry or exit stroke that looks as though it is cupping a portion of a very small circle.

INTERLINEAR The space between lines of writing.

KICK-LEG The lower diagonal stroke of K or R.

LETTER SLANT The forward tilt of an alphabet. 0° is considered to be upright.

LIGHTFAST Retains its original colour when exposed to daylight over a period of time. Artist-quality materials are rated for lightfastness.

LIGNIN A component of plant cells that may contribute to the degradation of paper over time.

LOWERCASE Letters, often with ascenders and descenders, that are used to accompany capitals; also called minuscules.

MAJUSCULES Uppercase or capital letters (A, B, C).

MINUSCULES Lowercase letters (a, b, c).

MONOCASE A complete alphabet that does not have separate upper and lower cases.

MONOLINE A tool or letter form with a single line width; without thicks and thins.

MOUNTAIN The highest points of an M.

NIB WIDTHS Used to determine the x-height, ascender and descender of calligraphic alphabets.

PEN ANGLE (FLAT, STEEPEN) The angle of the broad-edged pen nib relative to the baseline. A flat pen angle (0°) is parallel to the baseline. As you rotate the pen anticlockwise, the pen angle steepens. A change in pen angle is sometimes necessary to make strokes of correct weight or thickness.

PEN MANIPULATION While writing, the broad-edged pen is rotated between the thumb and forefinger in order to vary the width of the stroke.

PERMANENT Refers to waterproof writing fluid in a pen or marker.

PH NEUTRAL Neither acidic nor alkaline; having a pH value of 7 on a scale of 0–14.

PIGMENTED Refers to the quality of the colour source used in writing fluid; usually means it is lightfast.

PRESSURE Deliberate stress applied to the writing tool and against the writing surface to make a thicker stroke.

PRESSURE–RELEASE–PRESSURE A technique to make the beginning and end of a stroke heavier and the midsection of the same stroke lighter.

RETRACE Go over the same line or stroke again with the writing tool.

SANS SERIF Without visible entry and exit strokes.

SERIF An entry or exit stroke.

SHADING In this book, strokes made thicker by filling in an outlined area. Traditionally, shading was added to pointed pen scripts, by increasing pressure on a flexible pointed nib.

STAMP Leave an impression by pressing an inked object against the paper surface.

STROKE A section of a letter made without lifting the writing tool off the paper.

THICKS AND THINS Contrasting line widths within a letter; usually in reference to calligraphy.

TOOTH SERIF A short, tapered, manipulated stroke that hangs down from the tops of letters C, E, F, G and S.

UPPERCASE Capital or majuscule letters.

UPRIGHT 0° letter slant.

VALLEY The lowest points of a V or W.

VERSALS Decorative letters traditionally used in manuscripts at the beginning of chapters or paragraphs.

VERTICALS Downstrokes.

X-HEIGHT The height of the body of a lowercase letter, excluding ascenders and descenders.

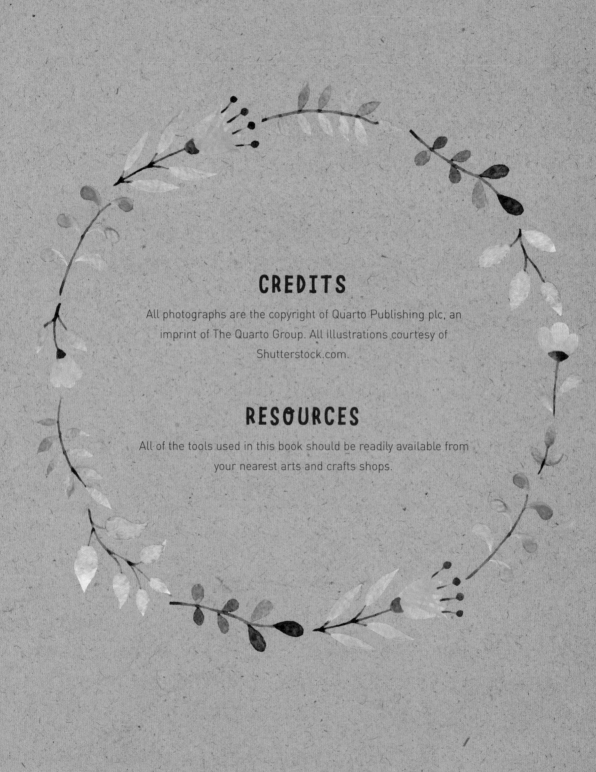

CREDITS

RESOURCES

All of the tools used in this book should be readily available from your nearest arts and crafts shops.